KNOWLEDGE ENCYCLOPEDIA

INVENTIONS & DISCOVERIES

Wonder House

(An imprint of Prakash Books)

contact@wonderhousebooks.com

Disclaimer: The information contained in this encyclopedia has been collated with inputs from subject experts. All information contained herein is true to the best of the Publisher's knowledge.

ISBN : 9789354404191

Table of Contents

Electronics & Communication

Inventions in Motion

Medical Inventions

ANCIENT
CIVILISATIONS

ARMS AND THE **MAN**

Human beings did not always walk on two feet. Our early ancestors walked on all fours. **Fossils** and other discoveries made by archaeologists show that our ape-like forefathers only began to walk upright between six- and three-million years ago. Once their arms were free, they were able to learn and do things that had never before been possible.

With the free use of arms, early human beings became smarter at handling things. Their creativity, combined with a natural curiosity, opened up a brave new world of inventions and discoveries for them! So what were their greatest finds? Who were the brightest inventors? Read on to discover more about the inventions of ancient civilisations.

▼ *Neanderthals were some of the first human beings to walk on two feet*

Material Progress

Look at any timeline of human history and you will notice that historians track human progress in terms of when certain materials were invented and used. Glass, paper, mortar, metals, and cloth are all a part of this timeline. Some materials are so important to us that historical periods have been named after them. The Stone Age, the Bronze Age and the Iron Age are classified according to when stone, bronze, and iron were used to create tools and technologies.

⊛ Incredible Individuals

Over 3 million years ago, the ancestors of humans began making stone tools. Among these early inventors was East Africa's *Australopithecus afarensis*. The most popular member of this species is Lucy. She was discovered by Donald Johanson and Tom Gray in 1974 in Hadar, Ethiopia. While Lucy was not the first to be discovered, her discovery revolutionised our understanding of human evolution; most importantly, that our brain size increased after we became **bipedal**

◀ *Bone fragments of Lucy, who lived some 3.2 million years ago*

2.58 MILLION YEARS AGO	c. 1.5 MILLION YEARS AGO	600,000 YEARS AGO	500,000 YEARS AGO	c. 170,000 YEARS AGO
This marked the start of the Palaeolithic Period, or the Old Stone Age. However, the world's earliest stone tools were even older. They belonged to **proto humans** who lived 3.3 million years ago, near Lake Turkana in East Africa.	Evidence shows that humans used fire for light, warmth, and to keep insects and predators away.	The earliest known man-made hearth or fireplace lay inside the Qesem Cave in Israel. About 15–20 people may have lived there and used fire for cooking. In fact, cooking food regularly may have played a role in expanding the brain!	In England, a Stone Age horse was discovered with a hole in its shoulder bone, made by a wooden spear. The oldest stone-tipped spears were seen in South Africa.	Humans began covering their bodies with clothes at this point. The first lice belong to the same time. Do you think there is a connection between the invention of clothes and the evolution of lice?

▶ *Lake Turkana lies in Africa's Great Rift Valley, often considered the cradle of civilisation*

▶ *Australopithecus afarensis looked part-ape and part-human*

Breakthroughs by Early Humans

Learning human history is not easy. Time, climate, and changing circumstances have destroyed many ancient artefacts. The Stone Age is regarded as the period in history when—across the world—early human tribes were using tools of wood, bone, and stone. Over time, humans have used many types of amazing materials to invent complex structures that made their lives comfortable, efficient, and sophisticated.

In Real Life

Do you think that only humans hunted animals with spears? Then you will be amazed by the videos of a group of chimpanzees in Africa that use spears to hunt galagos. Researchers have been able to spot the chimps hunting them about 22 times!

▶ *Galagos, also called bush babies, are smaller primates hunted by these chimps*

c. 26,000 BCE

Clay was used to make figurines, such as the Venus of Dolni Vestonice. She even bore the fingerprints of an ancient human child who held her!

◀ *The Venus of Dolni Vestonice, the oldest known clay figurine*

18,000 BCE

Clay vessels were made by early humans. Some of the oldest clay pots were found in Xianrendong Cave in China.

c. 6,000 BCE

Bricks were used to make the world's first cities. The ruins at Jericho, Turkey, belong to the oldest known city in our knowledge.

5,550–5,000 BCE

Ancient Egyptians invented linen cloth, spindles, and looms. Ancient Indians discovered the uses of cotton. Metal daggers were created.

◀ *Sun-dried bricks were made in Ur, an ancient city in Mesopotamia in c. 4,000 BCE*

All That Glitters

The Copper Age, also called the Chalcolithic Age, began 9,000–11,000 years ago. It is dated from around 4,000–2,000 BCE. It was the first time that humans began using metals. Early humans found that by heating copper, you could make it less hard and more malleable. This meant that they could beat it, melt it, mould it, and even mix it with other metals to make it stronger. Copper was easily mined and more durable than stone-made objects. Experimentation with copper led to the first metalwork technologies and the first smiths in the world.

▲ *A bell beaker from Central Europe dating back to the Copper Age*

▲ *Copper in its natural form*

The Bronze Rush

The Copper Age melts into the Bronze Age around 3,000 BCE. The Bronze Age began in Greece and China with the discovery of **alloys**. As different cultures learned the science of melting metals together, so the age spread across the globe. For instance, the Bronze Age in some parts of Africa began as late as the 1st millennium BCE.

Bronze is a yellowish alloy of copper and tin. It was used to make weapons, vessels, jewellery, statues, and heaps of other things. As demand for bronze grew, people looked far and wide for new sources of tin, leading to various explorations!

In Real Life

It is generally agreed that gold was the first metal to be discovered by humans. But it turned out to be too soft, too rare, and too expensive for practical daily use. Soon, the knowledge and skill of purifying and fashioning gold also became greatly valued. This is especially seen in ancient Egypt. Discovered in 1922, the tomb of the late Bronze Age pharaoh **Tutankhamun** is a hoard of golden treasures. His expressive funeral mask in particular is an example of the Egyptians' unparalleled craftsmanship.

Necklaces, plates, and rings from a Bronze Age hoard in Denmark

Bronze Age Leaps

After the invention of the wheel and the sailing ship, the first chariots appeared. Trading began, as metals were exchanged for wines and oils. Mathematics became more complex, leading to breakthroughs in astronomy and to improved weights and measures. People could now build spectacular structures like pyramids, temples, and ziggurats. Knowledge poured in from far-off regions. This included different ways of cooking and preserving foods.

▲ *Gold bull-headed bracelet from Bronze Age Transylvania*

▲ *A carving of a Sumerian war chariot*

▲ *An iron dagger from Anatolia, possibly the first country ever to use iron weapons beginning from around 2,000 BCE*

▶ *Bronze and Iron Age weapons from Romania*

▼ *The Ziggurat of Ur in Iraq, originally a temple*

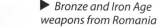

Iron Man

Over 1,200–300 BCE, iron replaced bronze as the metal of choice. Around 900 BCE, the Egyptians were the first to alloy iron with carbon to create the much lighter and stronger steel. Iron and steel weapons gave civilisations in Greece and Rome a huge advantage. This caused large-scale wars and migrations. Several kingdoms rose and faded during the Iron Age.

The secret of smelting iron ore to fashion tools was a technological breakthrough of the Hittite people of Anatolia

Black Sea
Istanbul
ANATOLIA (MODERN TURKEY)
Pontus
Phrygia
Hatti
Urartu
Cappadocia
Lydia
Hurri
Caria
Mitanni
Lycia
Iraq
Mediterranean Sea
Syria

Exploration and Invention

The Bronze Age saw an explosion of action across the globe. This was largely inspired by the need for metals such as tin, which was needed to make bronze. In the process, people travelled to and explored faraway lands. As they travelled, new trade routes were established. In addition, the means for journeying abroad were created, with inventions such as the wheel and the sailboat. As knowledge passed between cultures, human civilisation profited and progressed.

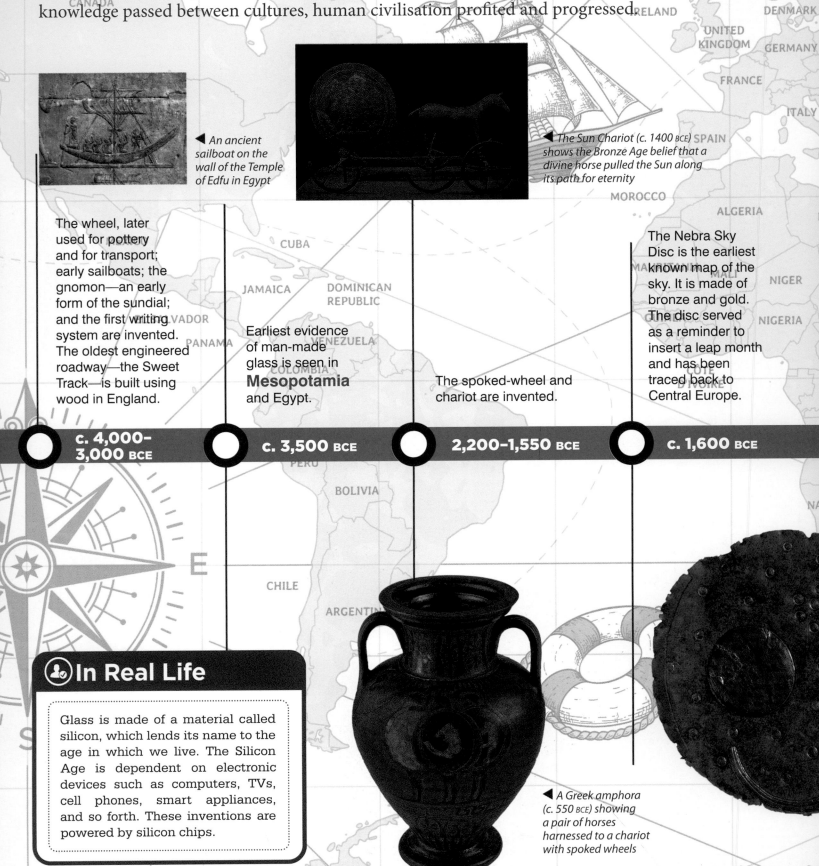

◀ *An ancient sailboat on the wall of the Temple of Edfu in Egypt*

◀ *The Sun Chariot (c. 1400 BCE) shows the Bronze Age belief that a divine horse pulled the Sun along its path for eternity*

The wheel, later used for pottery and for transport; early sailboats; the gnomon—an early form of the sundial; and the first writing system are invented. The oldest engineered roadway—the Sweet Track—is built using wood in England.

Earliest evidence of man-made glass is seen in **Mesopotamia** and Egypt.

The spoked-wheel and chariot are invented.

The Nebra Sky Disc is the earliest known map of the sky. It is made of bronze and gold. The disc served as a reminder to insert a leap month and has been traced back to Central Europe.

● **c. 4,000–3,000 BCE**

● **c. 3,500 BCE**

● **2,200–1,550 BCE**

● **c. 1,600 BCE**

In Real Life

Glass is made of a material called silicon, which lends its name to the age in which we live. The Silicon Age is dependent on electronic devices such as computers, TVs, cell phones, smart appliances, and so forth. These inventions are powered by silicon chips.

◀ *A Greek amphora (c. 550 BCE) showing a pair of horses harnessed to a chariot with spoked wheels*

Breakthroughs of the Bronze Age

As trade and knowledge grew, record-keeping became necessary. Thus, scripts were invented in the Bronze Age. Cuneiform, the earliest known form of writing, developed in ancient Sumeria. It was considered a gift from the god, Enlil. The Chinese developed their script around 1,600–1,046 BCE by throwing oracle bones. The cracks in the bones were considered the word of god and set down by writers.

▲ *The world's oldest coin, the Lydian Lion, is made of electrum, a mix of gold and silver. The Lydians may have been the first people to use gold and silver coins*

The first paved trackway called diolkos is built in ancient Greece. It is a line of grooved paving stones connecting two seaports. Goods 'trains' are hauled across it to save shipping costs. Light warships are also transported over the diolkos.

The first battery is made by Parthians in an area that lies in present-day Baghdad. It is made of clay jars filled with vinegar. Inside each jar is a copper cylinder with an iron rod on top. This early type of battery is most likely used to electroplate silver, which stops it from going black.

Cai Lun invents paper.

| **600** BCE | **500–400** BCE | **250** BCE | **105** BCE |

◀ *The Nebra Sky Disc shows the Sun, Moon, and the Pleiades constellation of stars*

▶ *An old gnomon—the projecting piece on a sundial—from the 7th century Sui dynasty in China*

Iron Age Inventors

The creators of the Iron Age lived so long ago, it is no surprise we know little about them. What we do know comes mostly through legends—stories that may or may not be true.

 ## Archimedes of Syracuse (c. 287-212 BCE)

The story goes that King Hieron II of Syracuse had a goldsmith make him a crown of pure gold. The king suspected, however, that the goldsmith mixed some silver into the crown. King Hieron commanded Archimedes to discover the truth. Though baffled at first, Archimedes found inspiration while taking a bath. As he sank into the bathtub, he saw his body displace a certain volume of water. He realised that you could identify pure metals based on how much water they displaced. He developed this observation into a mathematical concept called the Archimedes's Principle.

▲ *A bust of Archimedes of Syracuse*

Archimedes made several more contributions to mathematics. He invented a device for raising water called the Archimedes Screw. This is still used in many countries today. He was also a gifted engineer who built the defence and war machines of Syracuse. Tragically, he was killed by Roman soldiers when the army of General Marcus Claudius Marcellus sacked the city.

▶ *The Claw of Archimedes was a war machine meant to destroy enemy ships from the city's walls*

Cai Lun of China (c. 62-121 CE)

At the time, Chinese people used silk or bamboo pieces to write upon. Silk was expensive and bamboo was heavy. Cai Lun, an official of the imperial palace, used mashed up bark, hemp, rags, and fishing net to create paper, which was a new writing surface. His assistant Zu Bo improved the quality of paper and soon its popularity spread across the world.

Despite his brilliance, Cai Lun became involved in court politics and fell out of favour with the emperor. When summoned to a public trial, he took a bath, dressed in his finest clothes, and then ended his life by drinking poison.

▲ *The ancient Chinese process of papermaking, as outlined by Cai Lun*

Hero of Alexandria (lived c. 62 CE)

Hero, or Heron, was a mathematician and engineer of Egypt, then a part of the Roman Empire. He left behind many books on math, mechanics, and logic that are still studied today. Hero enjoyed inventing mechanical novelties such as singing birds and puppets that showcased his theories. He built a fire engine, a water-powered organ, the first syringe, and the first coin-operated machine. He even created a fountain that ran on a type of electricity.

Hero's most famous invention is the aeolipile, the world's first steam engine. However, no one understood its importance at the time. It took civilisation almost 2,000 years to rediscover and use the steam engine to make automated machines and vehicles.

▲ *Although most descriptions and ideas of Heron's work were lost, some of them are still kept in Arabic manuscripts*

▲ *A 16th century model of the aeolipile*

Hero's Aeolipile

Hero's aeolipile was a steam turbine described in his book *Pneumatica*. It was a hollow sphere mounted on a pair of hollow tubes in a way that it was able to turn when steam was let into the sphere through the hollow tubes from a cauldron. Near its middle, the aeolipile had bent tubes that let steam escape and allowed the sphere to revolve in place.

Isn't It Amazing!

In order to recognise and appreciate the contributions of Cai Lun and Archimedes, the modern scientific world named two craters on the Moon in their honour.

◀ *The Archimedes Screw is a device that raises water when a lever is turned. It is still used in some countries, especially for irrigation*

Iron Age Leaders and Thinkers

Apart from inventors, the Iron Age also saw the rise of many deep thinkers and leaders. These people are known today for their contributions to law, philosophy, governance, and abstract science.

▼ *The School of Athens, a fresco at the Vatican, represents philosophy. It depicts some of the most celebrated minds of ancient and medieval times, including Aristotle, Plato, the amazing Hypatia, Ibn-Rushd, Zoroaster, and Alexander the Great. The pioneering mathematicians Euclid, Pythagoras, and Archimedes are also shown. Socrates, Epicurus, Zeno, and Diogenes, each of whom founded a new branch of philosophy, are some other famous figures in this painting*

Chanakya (c. 350–275 BCE)

Chanakya was a teacher and political genius in ancient India. Frustrated with corruption in his country, Chanakya put forth his own ideas and methods for an ideal government. His clever ideas helped his disciple Chandragupta become emperor and establish the powerful Mauryan dynasty.

Chanakya also defeated the army of Alexander the Great at Gandhara—in modern Afghanistan—and forced them to turn back. He put down his great knowledge in the *Arthashastra*, a pioneering book on diplomacy, war, law, taxes, prison, coinage, industry, trade, administration, spies, and other topics. It is mainly owing to Chanakya that the Mauryan empire—from Chandragupta to Emperor Ashoka—became a model of efficient governance.

▲ *Coins of the Mauryan empire*

▲ *A fragment of the Arthashastra*

▲ *Euclid's name was derived from the Greek word which means 'Good Glory'*

Euclid (born c. 300 BCE)

Very little is known about the Greek mathematician Euclid, though he left behind some amazing mathematical work in his treatise, *Elements*. Euclid lived and taught in Alexandria, Egypt, during the reign of Ptolemy I Soter during 323–285 BCE. His treatise has continuously impacted human life since the time it was written. Except for the *Bible*, it is perhaps the most translated, published, and studied book in the Western world. Euclid's treatise was the main source of geometric knowledge and reasoning until non-Euclidean geometry came up 2000 years later!

Sammu-ramat (9th century BCE)

The legendary Sammu-ramat or Semiramis is the first known woman to rule an empire. She came to the throne in 811 BCE upon the death of her husband Shamshi-Adad V. At the time, **Assyria** was poor and weak owing to the late king's mismanagement. Queen Sammu-ramat took the reins of the kingdom and brought stability back to Assyria. Among her many great achievements was the building of the city Babylon, by the River Euphrates. Sammu-ramat led armies to put down uprisings in Persia and Africa, and even to invade India. So heroically did she fight and rule that the inscriptions of the time place her on par with the male rulers. In the years after her death, legends claimed her to be the daughter of a goddess!

▲ *Sammu-ramat fighting a lion*

⊛ Incredible Individuals

In 811 BCE, the Neo-Assyrian Empire had the largest territory in the world. It stretched in a bulging triangle between the Mediterranean Sea, Black Sea and Persian Gulf. Egypt and parts of Arabia and North Africa were also a part of this vast empire. When a civil war overtook its royal family, Queen Sammu-ramat rose to power.

Blocks of Civilisation

Around 4,000 BCE, the Sumerians were the first civilisation to build cities across their land. With names like Kish, Lagash, Umma, Eridu, and Uruk, these urban centres had temples, schools, and the tallest buildings ever seen. Like modern cities, they employed huge numbers of people, including carpenters, butchers, smiths, **scribes**, priests, bricklayers, brewers, potters, weavers, jewellers, and even hairdressers. As with other forms of human progress, cities would have been impossible without the invention of certain material technologies.

Moulding the Earth

Clay is one of the earliest materials exploited by humans. Different communities invented their own methods of using clay to advance civilisation. As a result, the remains of unique styles of earthenware can help us identify changing civilisations, even in the same region.

All forms of long-lasting pottery require the clay to be baked in an oven. If a vessel is made with only sun-dried clay, it cannot hold any liquid. But if it is heated (fired) in a kiln, to at least 500°C, irreversible chemical changes will occur within the clay to make the material stronger.

▲ Aqueducts are ancient structures that carried water to fields and cities. Many of them required brick and clay

The Appearance of Clay

Variations in the kiln and in firing give amazingly different kinds of pottery. Some ancient inventions in clay-based technologies include terracotta, ceramic, stoneware, porcelain, and china. Even in modern times, clay arts require much knowledge and skill, and the best clay pieces can be identified by region and artist. Clay was also used as an ingredient to make stronger building materials.

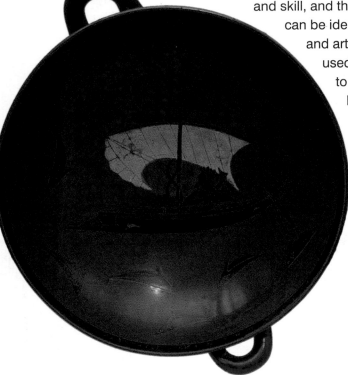

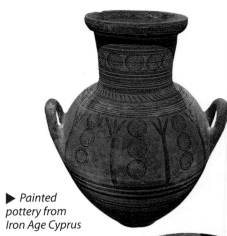

▶ Painted pottery from Iron Age Cyprus

▶ Shi Huangdi was China's first emperor. His tomb contains a vast army of terracotta soldiers

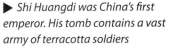
◀ The Greek god of grapes and wine, Dionysus, in a ship sailing among dolphins; black-figure pottery from Mycenaean Greece, c. 530 BCE

Brick by Brick

The invention of bricks allowed humans to build the first cities. The earliest bricks were sun-dried blocks of clay mixed with things like straw and shale. In the Mesopotamian city of Ur—roughly modern-day Iraq—sun-baked bricks were used to build the first true arch. This happened during 4,000 BCE. Eventually, people discovered the right mix of earthy ingredients to make the strongest bricks. They also fired bricks in kilns to make them more long-lasting.

In 210 BCE, engineers used both fired and sun-dried bricks to build the Great Wall of China. By 600 BCE, the Babylonians and Assyrians were adding a glaze or enamel to make coloured bricks. It is unfortunate that some of this ancient technology, the creation of certain blue glazes in particular, has been lost and cannot be recreated today.

▲ Brick ruins of a reservoir in Gujarat, India, which was part of the Indus Valley Civilisation

▼ Remains of an ancient Roman apartment block built with bricks

Cementing Success

Mortar is a slushy mix that is layered into the gaps between bricks or stones. It hardens in the air and holds the construction together more securely. Mortar is made of sand, water, and some kind of binder, such as lime. Ancient Egyptians developed the earliest known mortar in about 4,000 BCE. This was a soft paste of gypsum (plaster) and sand. The Romans used a slightly more advanced method to create lime mortars.

▲ *Many experts believe that the spectacular pyramids of Egypt had some type of mortar that held the stones together*

Roman Cement

About 2,000 years ago, the ancient Greeks and Romans invented a type of cement that used lime and volcanic ash. These two compounds reacted in the presence of water to form a hard mass. The mix set very slowly and took centuries to harden completely. As a result, many Roman structures are still standing today, though they were built way back in the Iron Age. In comparison, some of our modern mortars used in bridges, roads, and buildings crumble in 50–100 years.

▲ *In 79 CE, a volcanic eruption covered the ancient Roman city of Pompeii in lava. The cooling rock preserved the streets and buildings, including signs on shop fronts and Iron Age graffiti*

Monument for the Ages

The word cement comes from the Latin word 'caementum', which referred to stone chips, like the ones used to make Roman mortar. It did not refer to the cement mixture itself. Most buildings in Rome made use of multiple materials to create comfortable homes and striking landmarks. For instance, the famous Pantheon of Rome was constructed in 123 CE using brick, but had an amazing dome of concrete that stretched across 43 m.

▲ *The Basilica of Maxentius is a marvel of Roman engineering and would have been impossible without mortar*

▲ *Bathing was a social activity in Roman times. Ancient Roman baths were large constructions that required mortar*

Glued Together

Our ancestors created glue from natural materials as far back as 200,000 BCE. Natural glues were used for ceremonies and decorations around 6,000 years ago, and to fix axes and arrow tips about 5,200 years back. Later, stronger glues were invented by boiling the bones, hides, and other parts of animals.

🔍 Animal Glue

Ancient Egyptians are thought to have first discovered the use of animal glue to make furniture. These were usually made only for royal and wealthy Egyptians who could afford them. As far back as 2,500 years, the tombs of pharaohs were laden with laminated woodwork created by gluing the pieces together.

▲ *Pharaoh's chair in the Museum of Egyptian Antiques*

🔍 Adhesives

Did you know the word adhesive can be used for any material that binds things together? This includes cement, glue, paste, mucilage, starch, and other substances you wouldn't normally call 'sticky'. About 3,500 years ago, Egyptians were making papyrus, a writing surface, out of reed fibres glued together with flour paste.

◀ *This papyrus painting shows the pharaoh hunting a flock of birds as they rise above aquatic reeds*

🔍 The Many Uses of Glue

By Greek and Roman times, glue had become commonplace and was used for small jobs as well as for large building requirements. Chinese inventors at the time tried out adhesives made from fish, ox, and stag horns. They used glue not just for sticking things together but also to preserve paintings and for medical purposes.

▶ *Ancient Roman mosaics were made by gluing pieces of tiles in intricate patterns*

👤✓ In Real Life

Collagen is a protein found in the skin and bones of animals. Amazingly, both glue and gelatine—from which jellies are made—were created by boiling collagen! Pure collagen mildly treated with acids or hot water gives gelatine. Less pure collagen, vigorously treated the same way, will produce sticky, dark animal glue.

💡 Isn't It Amazing!

One square inch of modern super glue can hold around one ton of weight. To give you some idea, a small car weighs about 1.5 tonnes.

To Spin a Yarn

Clothes were first worn by proto humans called Neanderthals. They used animal hides to cover themselves and to show off their status! Then came the **Cro-Magnons**, who used needle-like tools to punch holes into hides and lace them up again.

▶ *Prehistoric clothes of Otzi, the Iceman*

🔍 Otzi the Iceman

Otzi the Iceman is a 5,300-year-old human who showed us what prehistoric fashion was like. His clothes were made from the skins, bones, horns, and feathers of six types of animals. His attire also had leaves, wood, and fibre from 17 different trees.

🔍 A New Set of Threads

Felt is the name given to the first man-made cloth; that is, not leather or fur, but real fabric. Felt is made by matting, condensing, and pressing natural fibres together. It was invented well before spinning, weaving, and knitting.

The Sumerians believed that it was Urnamman of Lagash, who discovered the secret of felt-making. In time, many different techniques of felting were invented.

◀ *A felt hat from the Loulan kingdom of Iron Age China*

🔍 Weaving

The oldest bit of woven cloth dates to the 7th millennium BCE. It was used for wrapping the dead in Anatolia (present-day Turkey). Nalbinding, an early type of knitting, was seen soon after, around 6,500 BCE.

In Japan, weaving was well established by 5,500 BCE. Painted pottery from this time shows people wearing clothes. As civilisations discovered new fibres, they invented more ways of creating textiles.

👤✓ In Real Life

Felt is still used today by nomadic people to create rugs, tents, and clothes. You have most likely seen felt in your arts and crafts classes.

▲ *Kirghiz nomads shifting their felt home*

💡 Isn't It Amazing!

A 50,000-year-old needle is the oldest sewing tool in existence. But it is not like any sewing needle we see today. Instead, it is made from the bone of a large bird and has a bit of twine still attached to it.

▶ *Denisova Cave in Siberia, Russia is a treasure trove of finds on early humans, including the world's oldest sewing needle*

🔍 Discovery of Amazing Fibres

Linen was made by Egyptians around 4,500 BCE. It was first used for bandaging mummies. Egyptians also tried out cloths made of rush, reed, palm, and papyrus; however, they considered animal fibres to be impure and taboo. Cotton was in use in ancient India by the 5th millennium BCE. Silk production began in China, probably around 5,000–3,000 BCE. Wool was used after sheep breeding took off in 3,000 BCE.

| Egyptian Pharaoh | Egyptian Queen | Greek man | Greek woman | Roman man in a toga | Roman woman |

▲ *Ancient robes of different civilisations*

🔍 The Silk Road

This was a cross-continental east-west network that allowed merchants to exchange luxury goods. It brought great wealth to civilisations across China, India, Egypt, Central Asia, and Rome.

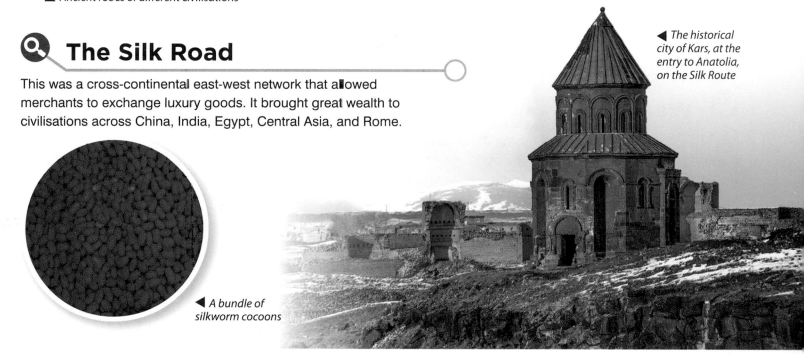

◀ *The historical city of Kars, at the entry to Anatolia, on the Silk Route*

◀ *A bundle of silkworm cocoons*

🔍 Loose Ends

Spinning is the word for pulling and twisting raw fibre into thread. Surprisingly though, spinning seems to have been invented after weaving. Around the time the Egyptians were producing linen, they invented the drop spindle, hand-to-hand spinning, and rolling the yarn on the thigh. They also knew of the horizontal ground loom and the vertical two-beam loom, both of which came from Asia.

▼ *The Egyptian drop spindle*

Fiercest Battle Inventions

Humans have fought each other since the dawn of our time on this planet. The earliest records of war, however, date from 2,700 BCE, when the Sumerian king Enmebaragesi fought and looted the **Elamite** people.

Over time, the need to wage successful wars brought amazing leaps in technology, science, and law. It also gave rise to awe-inspiring weapons that struck fear in the hearts of enemies.

▲ An Assyrian charioteer and archer with shield bearers, possibly from an Iron Age battle against the Elamite city, Hamaru

🔍 Spearheading the Charge

▲ Philip II of Macedon developed the pike into the elongated sarissa, which was 4–6.5 m long. This gave his army of hoplites an offensive and defensive advantage

Originally a throwing weapon from Stone Age times, the spear evolved into different forms and functions. By 3,000 BCE, Sumerian armies were charging in close-knit groups called phalanxes. They used the spear to thrust into the enemy at close range.

The Greeks refined the spear into a 2–3 m long weapon called the pike.

◀ Philip's son, Alexander the Great, used sarissa-bearing armies to conquer an empire

▶ The Romans used a long, heavy javelin called pilum. This was thrown by foot soldiers and cavalry

◀ This amphora from 540–530 BCE shows Greek champion Hercules wielding a pike and shield

◀ The phalanx became a standard formation of the Roman infantry

To Fire at Will

The bow and arrow are prehistoric inventions. It is said that they were made for hunting nearly 64,000 years ago in South Africa. Bows were originally made of springy woods and strung with animal gut. Around 1,700 BCE, the composite bow was invented in various cultures of Asia. It was usually made of layers of wood, horns, and sinew glued together. By 1,000 CE, horse-riding archers in central Asia had invented the recurved bow. It had a wide W shape that allowed even short bows to shoot far-off targets.

◀ *Diana, Greek goddess of the hunt, painted with a recurved bow in her hands*

▶ *This Turkish composite bow was clearly a cherished possession—it is decorated with pigments, gold, silver, and ivory*

Amazing Arrows

Arrows were made of wood and tipped with sharp flint, hard wood, horn, or metal. The oldest arrow points came from Africa some 64,000 years ago and were made of bone. In the 3rd century BCE, weapon-makers of India invented an all-metal arrow. They also might have made metal bows, but these became popular only in the 17th century CE.

▲ *Pharaoh Tutankhamen shooting at his enemies; section of a wooden painting done around 1,327 BCE*

In Real Life

The amazing *urumi*, meaning 'curling sword', is a flexible whip-like sword from prehistoric southern India. It might have been used in the northern Mauryan Dynasty near 350–150 BCE. It can be seen today in the martial arts of southern India: *Kalaripayattu* and *Silambam*.

▲ *It takes years to master the use of the urumi*

The Hero's Club

A lethal bludgeon from the Bronze Age, the mace is the first weapon invented specifically for war. It was fashioned out of rock and could smash body and bone. Naturally, such a hefty weapon was not for everyone; it was mostly used by champions and kings. By 3,000 BCE, mace-heads were cast in elaborate shapes using copper at Mesopotamia, Syria, Palestine, and Egypt.

To Parry and Thrust

The sword became separate from the dagger during the Bronze Age. However, right up till Roman times, swords were still quite short and narrow. The technology for making true swords remained a mystery till medieval times.

▶ *A carving from 3100 BCE depicting Pharaoh Menes, the first ruler of a united Egypt. He is the earliest mace-bearing hero we know of by name*

▼ *A curved sword from Bronze Age Scandinavia*

Throw and Scatter

Not all weapons were for close-range use like the sword or the mace. There were many strong weapons invented for long-range combat like the crossbow or the catapult. Weapons like the caltrop were used in a clever manner to injure those on horseback.

Quick on the Trigger

The amazing repeating crossbow, the zhuge nu, was the first weapon to resemble modern automatic firing machines. The magazine atop the barrel held several pre-loaded arrows, which could be fired one after the other. This gave the soldier a deadly advantage over his opponent who fired more slowly, as he had to stop and reload an arrow after each shot.

So amazing was this invention, that it was seen in use during the war between China and Japan in 1894–1895. The development of the repeating crossbow is associated with Zhuge Liang, a brilliant military tactician of the Three Kingdoms period of China (220–280 CE). He developed a bow that could shoot many arrows at one time. Other accounts show that the repeating crossbow predates him.

▲ *The magazine and arrows of an ancient Chinese repeating crossbow*

Caltrops

Caltrops are small spiked weapons that are still used in modern warfare. Then, as now, they were scattered on the ground where they could fatally injure the enemies' horses and men. In 331 BCE, during the Battle of Gaugamela in modern Iraq, the Persians sowed the battlefield with caltrops to prevent Alexander the Great's troops from advancing. Although Alexander overcame them, he greatly admired the invention and adopted its use in later battles.

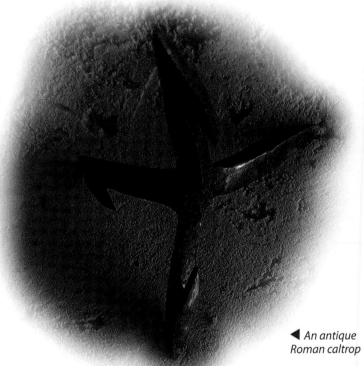

◄ *An antique Roman caltrop*

▲ *Caltrops were used in World War I to disable horses*

In Real Life

Developed versions of the caltrops were used as weapons during World War II. The US, British, and French officers would parachute into enemy territory and release caltrops across their runways. The caltrops punctured the tires of all the vehicles that moved on the runway and sabotaged the enemy's operations.

Boomerang

Though associated with Aboriginal Australians, the boomerang was a popular hunting tool throughout Africa and Europe in ancient times. Not all boomerangs are designed to return when thrown. Some of them are fashioned like axes and used in combat between warriors. The oldest boomerang yet known was carved from the tusk of a mammoth and dates back to 23,000 BCE. It was found in a cave in Poland.

▲ Egyptian hunting boomerangs decorated with gold; treasures from Pharaoh Tutankhamun's tomb

▼ The Roman ballista was an ancient missile weapon that launched either bolts or stones at a distant target

◀ The heavy, naturally curved bone of mammoths' tusks could be used to make boomerangs

A Giant Catapult

Used to launch heavy objects such as rocks and large spears at far-off enemies, the ballista was invented by the Greeks. It was then refined by the Romans during the 3rd and 4th centuries BCE. The largest ballista of this time could accurately lob 27 kg weights to a distance of 450 m.

▼ Later modifications to the ballista turned it into an enormous machine that could fling flaming missiles into enemy armies and strongholds

Mightier than the Sword

Though speaking comes naturally to all of us, writing has to be formally learned. But when did writing systems evolve? In the 4th millennium BCE, trade and wealth were expanding rapidly. People needed a way to track their bargains, monies, properties, and other details. Kings also needed such information, so they could exact taxes for making roads and war. The first scripts were most likely invented as memory aids and bookkeeping tools. But they soon flourished to express larger, bolder, newer ideas that would change the world over and over again.

▼ This giant cuneiform 'page' was inscribed into the side of a hill by order of the Persian King Xerxes in praise of the God Ahuramazda

▶ Sumerian cuneiform is the earliest writing we know of. This cone from 1,850 BCE records, 'Sin-kashid, mighty man, king of Uruk, king of the Amnanum, provider of the temple Eanna, built his royal palace'

▲ Ancient Egyptian scripts are called hieroglyphics, meaning 'sacred carvings'. You often see them on amazing murals accompanying gods and pharaohs

▼ Evidence of Chinese writing exists from 1,500 BCE, but it likely developed well before that. This tortoise shell shows a divination from the time of King Wu Ding (1,200 BCE)

▼ Hieroglyphic carvings at an ancient Egyptian temple

▼ One of the 12 clay tablets of the earliest known poem, 'The Epic of Gilgamesh', 2,003–1,595 BCE

Carved in Stone

The scripts of the 4th millennium BCE were etched on to clay tablets with a reed stylus. Sometimes, they were drawn with ink made of ground charcoal, powdered insects, plants, or natural pigments. People also wrote on bone, stone, wax tablets, animal skins, tanned leather, bark, and silk. Around 3,100–2,900 BCE, Egypt invented papyrus from reeds that grew by the River Nile. This was used in the form of washable, reusable scrolls, and to wrap mummies!

Around 104–105 CE, the imperial official Cai Lun showed his invention of paper to the Han emperor of China. It rapidly became the writing material of choice for the entire world.

▲ In ancient India, sacred and political texts would be recorded on strips of palm leaves tied together to form manuscripts

In Real Life

The invention of the alphabet powered most modern written languages. Most Western, Arabic, and Indian alphabets come from a system of writing popular in Syria in the 11th century BCE. The Greeks were the first to adapt it to their language, around 1,000–900 BCE.

◄ The Code of Hammurabi is a stone tablet from 2nd millennium BCE recording the laws and punishments of its Babylonian king

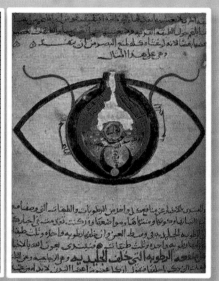

▲ Ancient alphabets: a Greek page from 'The Odyssey'; an Arabic medical page about the eye

▼ Some of the Dead Sea Scrolls (300 BCE– 200 CE), manuscripts of great importance to Christianity and Judaism, were written on thin, whitish leather

Which Way is North?

Did you know that Earth has two poles? What we think of as the top and bottom points of the planet are the geographic north and south poles, respectively. But, Earth also has magnetic north and south poles, which are hundreds of miles away from the true or geographic north and south. The compass, which is a magnetic device, will always point to the magnetic north pole. But when was it invented?

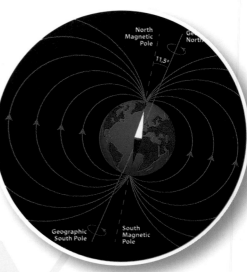

▶ Earth is a giant spinning magnet with moving magnetic poles and fixed geographic poles

⊛ Incredible Individuals

Chinese inventor Ma Jun (200–265 CE) built a chariot with a small statue atop that always pointed south. This clever contraption did not use magnets. It had a system of gears that turned the statue in the direction opposite to the chariot, but at the same angles. Thus, one could never be lost in a chaotic battlefield with such a tool.

Legend has it that the Qin dynasty (221–206 BCE) invented a south-pointing ship along similar lines. But it is more likely that the ship used magnets, which were well known to the Qin engineers.

🔍 Compass

Some scholars believe that the magnetic compass was invented by the Chinese during the 2nd–1st century BCE. Early magnetized needles were set on wood and floated in a basin of water. When the needle came to a standstill, its marked tip would point North-South. Records show a spoon-shaped compass dating from the ancient Han Dynasty. The magnetic spoon rested on a square bronze plate—representing Earth—that bore a circle—symbolizing heaven. The board was marked with constellations and astrological signs. The first Chinese emperor is said to have used such a divining board and compass in court to affirm his right to the throne! It would be several centuries more before the compass was put to practical use by travellers.

◀ Ma Jun's south-pointing chariot

💡 Isn't It Amazing!

If you had a compass 800,000 years ago, its needle would have pointed towards the southern hemisphere! Since its discovery in the early 19th century, the magnetic north has drifted over 966 km and continues to move every year. Scientists worry that the next pole swap could destroy our entire electric grid!

◀ This south-pointing spoon is a compass of the Chinese Han dynasty (202 BCE–220 CE)

A Gaze at Glass

Natural glass occurs when sand is hit by lightning or when molten lava cools rapidly. Humans used such glass, called obsidian, to make weapons, jewellery and money, long before they invented glass-making technologies. The Roman historian Pliny believed that glass was first made in 5,000 BCE by Phoenician merchants around Syria. However, the earliest real evidence of man-made glass comes from 3,500 BCE, from Egypt and Mesopotamia. People here were also the first to make glass vessels in 1,500 BCE.

▲ *Ancient arrowhead made of obsidian*

▲ *Ancient Egyptian coffin mask made of dark glass and wood*

🔍 Recipe for Glass

We know how Mesopotamians made glass from ritual-like instructions they left behind on clay tablets. The ingredients include sand, soda ash, and 'white plant', which is an unknown substance. Some truly amazing colours were added by using metallic oxides.

Copper and cobalt compounds gave the glass royal blue and turquoise blue tints that are still popular today. The earliest glass-making manual belongs to the amazing library of Nineveh built by Ashurbanipal (669–631 BCE), the last great king of ancient Assyria.

▶ *Tinted glass vessels from ancient Rome*

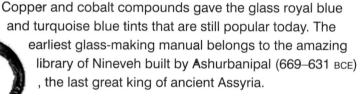

🔍 Glass-blowing

Only the very rich and powerful could afford to buy glass in the early days. This changed when Syrians invented glass-blowing at the end of the 1st century CE. Suddenly, it was easier, faster, and cost-effective to make glass. For the first time, ordinary people could afford to buy and enjoy the convenience and beauty of glass products.

◀ *Ancient Syrian glass flask*

▶ *Miniature glassware from the 18th dynasty of ancient Egypt*

▲ The Fertile Crescent was a sickle-shaped land that was the birthplace of a number of technological innovations

Creating Surplus

Historians often mark the beginning of civilisation as that crucial time when hunter-gatherers gave up wandering and began farming. Agricultural technologies allowed humans to literally reap the wealth of the earth. To farm successfully, we tamed rivers, mountains, and, of course, plants and animals. The farmers' labour and ingenuity created so much surplus that populations grew rapidly. With more people came specialised occupations and about 11,000 years of the most amazing advances in civilisation.

▲ The Egyptians invented the Nilometer in the 3rd century BCE. It is a measuring column that sunk into the river to check flood levels

◄ The first large network of dams and channels was created by Egypt's First Dynasty. It began in 3,100 BCE under King Menes and led to the formation of Lake Moeris, which is still around

9,500 BCE
The eight founding crops of agriculture—emmer and einkorn wheat, barley, peas, lentils, bitter vetch, chickpeas, and flax—are cultivated in the Fertile Crescent.

8,000 BCE
Agriculture begins in parts of the Americas as hunter-gatherers grow wild crops to broaden their food sources. Squash is one of these early crops.

6,000 BCE
Irrigation begins: the floodwaters of the Nile (in Egypt) and the rivers Tigris and Euphrates (in Meso-potamia) are diverted to the fields over July–December and then drained back into the rivers.

2,800 BCE
The first evidence of a ploughed field is seen at Kaliban-gan. The area was part of the Indus Valley Civilisation.

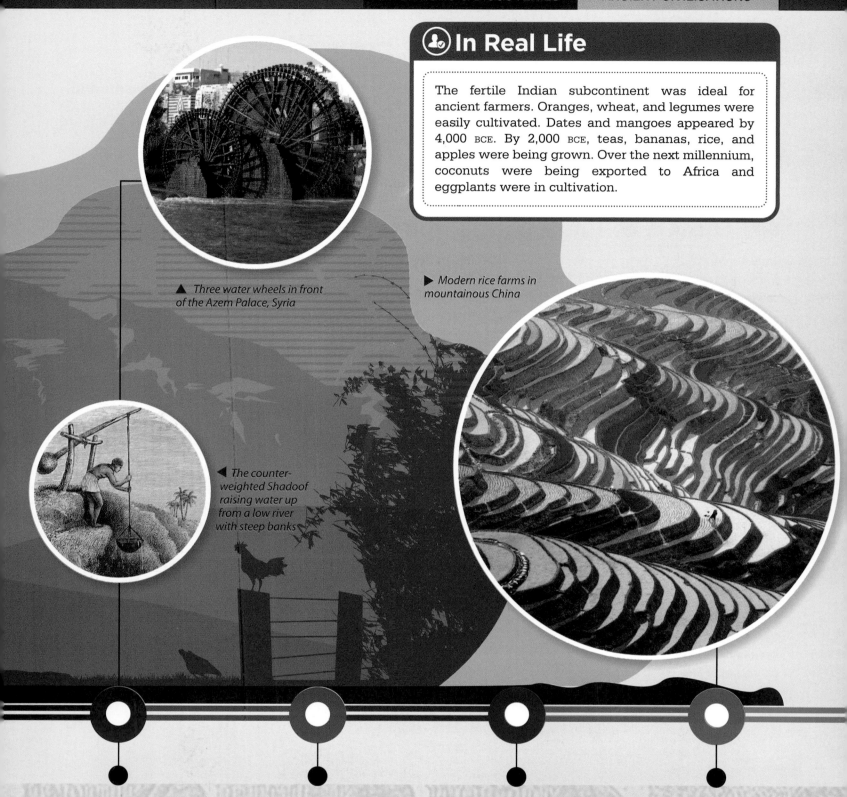

In Real Life

The fertile Indian subcontinent was ideal for ancient farmers. Oranges, wheat, and legumes were easily cultivated. Dates and mangoes appeared by 4,000 BCE. By 2,000 BCE, teas, bananas, rice, and apples were being grown. Over the next millennium, coconuts were being exported to Africa and eggplants were in cultivation.

▲ Three water wheels in front of the Azem Palace, Syria

▶ Modern rice farms in mountainous China

◀ The counter-weighted Shadoof raising water up from a low river with steep banks

1,700 BCE
When the river is not in flood, an invention called the Shadoof allows farmers to lift water for irrigating fields using a bucket. By 700 BCE, this is further eased by the invention of the water wheel, which required little human effort.

500 BCE
Greece uses crop rotation methods on large estates.

100 BCE
The Chinese invent the hydraulic-powered trip hammer to pound and polish grain.

100 CE
The Chinese invent the square-pallet chain pump. It is powered by a water-wheel or pulled by oxen. It raises water up into channels that irrigate farmland on high ground.

▶ A hydraulic-powered trip hammer

Preserving Food

While hunter-gatherers ate a variety of vegetables and meats depending on the season and their location, the farmers continued to eat the limited crops they planted. Farmers also suffered due to floods, droughts, and pest attacks, all of which could leave them starving. The need to overcome hunger and find variety in food led early man to invent numerous ways of cooking and storing foods.

🔍 The Art of Preserving Food

Early humans found varied ways to extend the shelf life of food. These included heating raw food, drying and smoking to remove water, pickling, fermentation, etc. Such measures served the twin benefits of preventing bacteria and yeast from spoiling food, while also introducing the early man to a variety of flavours and textures.

⭐ Incredible Individuals

It is said that Queen Cleopatra of Egypt ate pickles as part of her beauty diet. Julius Caesar fed pickles to his armies. He believed it gave them spiritual and physical strength. While that might have been just a belief, their army certainly conquered several kingdoms!

▲ *Pickling was known to the Mesopotamians as early as 2,400 BCE*

🔍 The Oldest Form of Cooking

In its earliest form, baking was done by dry-roasting grains or cooking a batter of water and cereals over fire. The Egyptians may have been the first to use the oven for baking. By c. 2,600 BCE, they were also using **leavening**—the raising agent in bread.

▶ *Funerary model of a bakery and brewery, from ancient Egypt's 11ᵗʰ dynasty*

◀ *A Syrian baking mould from 2ⁿᵈ millennium BCE shows goats and a cow being attacked by a lion*

🔍 A Fishy History

Fishing nets, spears, lines, and rods appeared in Egypt around 3,500 BCE. In Greece and Rome, surplus fish were stored in a fermented form called 'garum', a popular condiment.

A Pinch of Salt

First discovered around 6,050 BCE, salt was a valuable trade commodity. In China, peasant families would set aside a jar of salted vegetables every year. These were given to the daughter upon her marriage. The Chinese used salt not directly, but through condiments like soy sauce and fish paste. The Egyptians even used salt for funeral offerings. They mixed brine, that is, saltwater, with vinegar to form a sauce called 'oxalme', which was later used by the Romans.

▲ *The ancient Chinese way of boiling brine to produce salt*

A Dash of Sugar

A grass called sugar cane was refined into sugar c. 500 BCE in India. By c. 200 BCE, the crop was being grown in China. In c. 510 BCE, soldiers of the Persian king, Darius found 'reeds which produce honey without bees' near the Indus River. Sugar, like salt, is an excellent preservative. However, it also attracts moisture. Sugar water causes microorganisms to begin the fermentation process, which produces alcohol. It is likely that some form of the drink was discovered this way!

◀ *Sugar cane helps in 80 per cent of the world's sugar production*

In Real Life

In ancient Rome, salt was so valuable, it could be used in place of money. In fact, many Roman workers and soldiers were paid in salt. In Latin, the word salarium meant a payment made in salt. It gives us the modern word, salary.

▶ *Bolivia's Salar de Uyuni is the world's largest and highest salt flat. It is the remnant of a prehistoric lake*

Isn't It Amazing!

The Chinese discovered fermentation and distillation 9,000 years ago. They were probably the first people to drink alcohol.

EARTH
DISCOVERIES

MAPPING EARTH

Human beings began large-scale explorations of Earth some 4,000 years ago. The European Age of Discovery, however, began during the 15th century. During this time, Europeans strove to discover and colonise lands that could make them rich. Their explorations led to an increase in their knowledge of the New World, the polar regions, and the southern hemisphere. They discovered new ocean routes and islands. Many of their adventures led to scientific discoveries that revolutionised the world. Their commercial motives also led to empire building, war, prejudice, and slavery. In the 20th century, satellite images filled in details of the last unknown parts of Earth.

▼ A map of the world from 1733 shows nothing but water around the poles. The Arctic and Antarctic expeditions were dangerous adventures undertaken by only the hardiest, most determined explorers

The Adventures of Marco Polo

Italian merchant Marco Polo (1254–1324) introduced the fabled worlds of China and Asia to medieval Europe. Marco belonged to a family of jewel merchants who traded with Eastern nations. In 1271, he journeyed with his father and uncle (Niccolo and Maffeo Polo) to the powerful Mongol kingdom. Marco Polo was just 17 years old. Over the next 24 years, he would acquire incredible knowledge of Asia and Europe through his fantastic travels.

▲ *An 1867 mosaic of Marco Polo at the Palazzo Grimaldi Doria-Tursi (the Municipal Palace of Genoa)*

🔍 The Legendary Silk Road

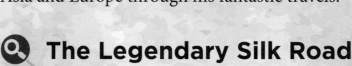

Carrying letters from the Pope to the Mongol Emperor Kublai Khan, Marco and his relatives journeyed through the wealthy city of Acre into south-eastern Turkey and northern Iran. They crossed hostile bandit-infested deserts and rested at Hormuz, a city on the Persian **Gulf**. The Polos then continued into Asia using the Silk Road.

The legendary Silk Road was a string of valuable trade routes across China, India, and the Mediterranean. Large convoys of wealth-laden caravans were a common sight here. They were often accompanied by armed cohorts to guard the riches. The Polos visited fabulous places like Khorasan, Badakhshan, Pamir, Kota, and even the Gobi Desert. Finally, in 1275, they reached Chengdu, where they met Kublai Khan at his summer palace.

▼ *Marco Polo's route from Venice (Italy) to Mongol China, then known as Cathay to the West*

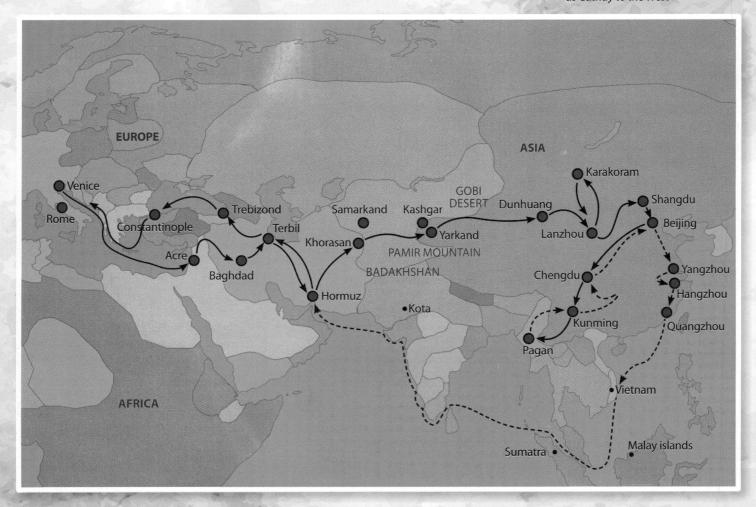

⭐ Incredible Individuals

Young Marco was amazed by the opulence of Mongol China. Nothing in Europe quite compared to it. The Khan's capital city, **Kinsay**, was large, clean, and organised. It had wide roads and extraordinary infrastructure—like the Grand Canal, which is, even today, the largest man-made waterway.
The food, the clothes, the people, and the animals were all new and fascinating to Marco. In his book, he wrote of rhinoceroses and crocodiles, which he thought were unicorns and giant, toothed serpents with "eyes bigger than a four penny loaf!"

▶ *An engraving of Marco Polo*

🔍 The Khan's Favourite

Marco was about 20 years old when he reached China. He would live there for another 17 years. He became a favourite of Kublai Khan, who loved listening to his stories of far-off lands. In fact, the emperor sent Marco to explore different parts of his own empire. Eventually, Marco held official posts at court. He even claimed to be the governor of Yangzhou for about three years.

🔍 Journey Home

Around 1290–1292, Kublai Khan sent a princess-bride to Argun Khan of Persia. She was accompanied by 600 courtiers and 14 ships. Reluctantly, he also allowed the Polos to leave in her train. They visited Vietnam, the Malay islands, and Sumatra, before reaching Persia. From there, the Polos travelled on to Trebizond (where they were badly robbed) and Constantinople. They reached home in Venice, in 1295.

▲ *Soon after his death in 1294, Kublai Khan was painted (as a younger man) by the Nepalese artist and astronomer Anige. This silk painting can be seen at the National Palace Museum in Taiwan*

🔍 Il Milione

In 1298, Marco Polo became a prisoner of war. That year, he narrated his stories to a fellow prisoner, Rustichello. The tales were published and became hugely popular. For the first time in centuries, Europeans learned what the East was really like. The amazing book, *Il Milione* is more commonly known as *The Travels of Marco Polo* in English.

👥 In Real Life

The maps that Marco Polo brought back from his journey influenced the development of **cartography** and are still used as a guide for undiscovered archaeological sites.

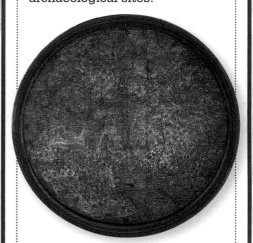

▲ *The 15th century monk Fra Mauro's map of the world—the most accurate map of that time—owed a great deal to a nautical map and a world map that Polo brought back from his travels*

▲ *Marco Polo passed away at the age of 70 in Venice. He lies buried at the Campo San Lorenzo*

China's Exploration of the 'West'

One of China's greatest admirals and diplomats, Zheng He (1371–1433) commanded seven epic sea voyages. He extended China's influence over the Indian ocean and parts of Africa and the Middle East.

🔍 Emperor Yongle's Mission

By 1368, the Mongol rulers of China had been overthrown. A new Ming dynasty held the throne. Zheng He was only 10 years old when his Mongol home was lost to war. Forced to join the Ming army, he grew into a strong and diplomatic warrior. By 1390, he had powerful friends in the imperial court. When the emperor wanted to conquer the 'Western Oceans', he chose Zheng He to lead the navy.

▲ *Statue of the Yongle Emperor in Ling En Hall of Changling tomb, in Ming Dynasty Tombs, Beijing*

🔍 The Indian Ocean

The first voyage, over 1405–1407, began with 62 ships and 27,800 men. Zheng He visited Champa (southern Vietnam), Siam (Thailand), Malacca, and Java. He then travelled to the wealthy port of Calicut in India and to Ceylon (Sri Lanka). In 1408–1409, Zheng He returned to India and Ceylon. However, he ended up in a battle with Ceylon's King Alagonakkara. Zheng He defeated the king and took him back as a prisoner to China.

◀ *A statue of Zheng He at the Quanzhou Maritime Museum*

▶ *A 17th century Chinese woodblock print of Zheng He's ships*

★ Incredible Individuals

Zheng He was born as Ma Sanbao to a Chinese Muslim family. His devout father made the Hajj **pilgrimage** to Mecca. Their name Ma is a Chinese word that comes from 'Muhammad'. Later in life, Zheng He became more interested in Buddhism.

▶ *Sculpture of a young Zheng He with his father Ma Hajji*

Arabia and Africa

In October 1409, Zheng He took to the seas again. He sailed all the way to Hormuz on the Persian Gulf. On his return in 1411, he touched the northern tip of Sumatra. During his fourth **expedition**, in 1413, he went farther down the Arabian coast to Dhofar (Oman) and Aden (Yemen). The mission took him to Mecca, Egypt, and to modern-day Somalia and Kenya. By 1415, Zheng He was back before the Chinese emperor. He brought **envoys** or **ambassadors** from more than 30 states to pay respect to the emperor.

The Final Forays

The fifth voyage, over 1417–1419, was to the Persian Gulf and East Africa. In 1421, the sixth voyage was launched to send foreign ambassadors home. Around this time, a new emperor came to power. He put a stop to these missions. However, Zheng He made one final voyage in the winter of 1431 to southeast Asia, India, the Persian Gulf, the Red Sea, and Eastern Africa. On the return trip, he passed away in Calicut in the spring of 1433.

◄ Indonesia issued special stamps to commemorate the 600th anniversary of Admiral Zheng He's voyage

Isn't It Amazing!

Zheng He's fleets carried priceless **lacquerware**, porcelains, and silks made by Ming craftsmen. These were traded at different ports for gems, spices, ivory, aromatics, herbs, and other valuable items. Zheng He even brought back a giraffe to China!

▲ The well-travelled giraffe of the Sultan of Bengal was originally brought from the Somali Ajuran Empire. It was eventually taken to China in the 13th year of the Yongle emperor

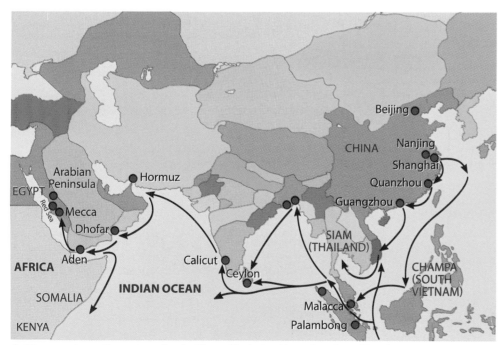

▲ The map shows the routes taken by Zheng He during his exploration of Southeast Asia, India, Middle East, and Africa

▲ Zheng He's tomb in Nanjing, China

A Passage to India

The infamous Portuguese navigator Vasco da Gama (1460–1524) opened up a new sea route from Europe to India. This took him around the Cape of Good Hope, which is located in the south of the continent of Africa. Its name comes from a belief of ancient travellers that India could be reached by sea from Europe. Vasco da Gama sailed for King Manuel I of Portugal, who wanted to control the riches of India.

▲ King Manuel I directs a kneeling Vasco da Gama to sail to India

The First Voyage: 1497–1499

Da Gama left Lisbon with four ships on 8 July 1497. After battling storms and scurvy, they sailed into Calicut on 20 May 1498. Calicut was then a wealthy port-city on India's western coast. Its powerful ruler, the Zamorin, courteously received the Portuguese sailors. But in return, da Gama offered cheap gifts. He even tried selling poor-quality items to the savvy city merchants. Naturally, people refused his offers and looked down upon him. A sulking da Gama left by the end of August, vowing revenge.

Isn't It Amazing!

On his first voyage, da Gama was away for over two years. He spent 300 days at sea and travelled about 39,000 km.

▲ An 1850 engraving shows da Gama greeting the Zamorin, the king of Calicut

In Real Life

Da Gama's ships carried stone pillars meant to mark 'discovered' territories, even though the regions were already inhabited by **indigenous** populations.

▲ Arriving from Lisbon, Portugal to Kochi, India

The Second Voyage: 1502–1503

Da Gama returned to India with an armed fleet, intent on wreaking havoc. He began by stealing the cargo of an Arab ship and setting its 200–400 passengers—men, women, and children—on fire! With the help of Cannore (now Kannur) and Cochin (now Kochi)—enemies of Calicut—he forced the Zamorin to agree to his terms. Da Gama sailed back to Portugal with shiploads of ill-gotten gains.

The Last Voyage: 1524 CE

In 1524, da Gama returned as the Portuguese Viceroy of India. However, he fell ill and died in Kochi. In 1538, his body was sent back to Portugal.

◀ Vasco da Gama's pillar in Kenya, to commemorate his 'discovery' of the land

The New World

The 15th century Italian explorer Christopher Columbus is often credited with discovering the Americas. However, many others were there before him—notably the Native Americans and the Vikings. Columbus's achievement was bringing the Americas into wider public consciousness. His ambition kicked off global territorial battles. In the same century, a Spanish **conquistador** named Vasco Nunez de Balboa established the first stable settlement in the New World and 'discovered' its eastern shores of the Pacific Ocean.

▲ In the 16th century, Italian explorer Amerigo Vespucci first realised that South America was a proper continent and not an extension of Asia. He thus called it the New World. He also discovered present-day Brazil

A Permanent Settlement

In 1510, Balboa, a failing planter and pig farmer in Haiti, escaped his creditors by hiding in a ship's barrel, along with his dog Leoncico! The ship brought him to the Spanish settlement of Uraba in modern Colombia. The settlement eventually moved to the **Isthmus** of Panama. There, they defeated 500 Native Americans led by chief Cemaco and established Santa Maria la Antigua del Darien, the first permanent settlement of Europeans on the American mainland.

◀ Columbus lands in the West Indies and claims the territory for imperial Spain, while ignoring the fact that the land was already home to many indigenous people

Panama and the Pacific

In 1515, Balboa sailed from Santa Maria to Acla, the narrowest part of the Isthmus of Panama. He was hunting for a rumoured gold-rich province. Balboa brought along 190 Spaniards and hundreds of porters. They travelled southwards through deep forests, crossing rivers and swamps, and ascending a mountain range. On 25 September 1513—though part of the travel record also states 27 September as the date—standing "silent, upon a peak in Darien", Balboa found himself looking at the Pacific Ocean.

The South Sea

▲ The modern Port of Balboa on the Panama Canal, built over the 19th and 20th centuries

A group led by Alonso Martin became the first to actually reach the Pacific shore. Balboa himself arrived on 29 September. He walked into the sea with a holy flag and a sword. Taking possession of the new sea for the King of Castille, he named it the Mar del Sur, or South Sea.

▶ A statue showing Vasco Nunez de Balboa claiming the South Sea

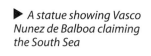

Shortcuts and Roundtrips

Sailing for the king of Spain, Ferdinand Magellan (1480–1521) was the first European to discover the sea route that goes below South America. The passage is named after him as the **Strait** of Magellan. It became Europe's shortcut to the Pacific Ocean. Magellan's ship—under the leadership of Juan Sebastian del Cano—was also the first to fully circumnavigate Earth.

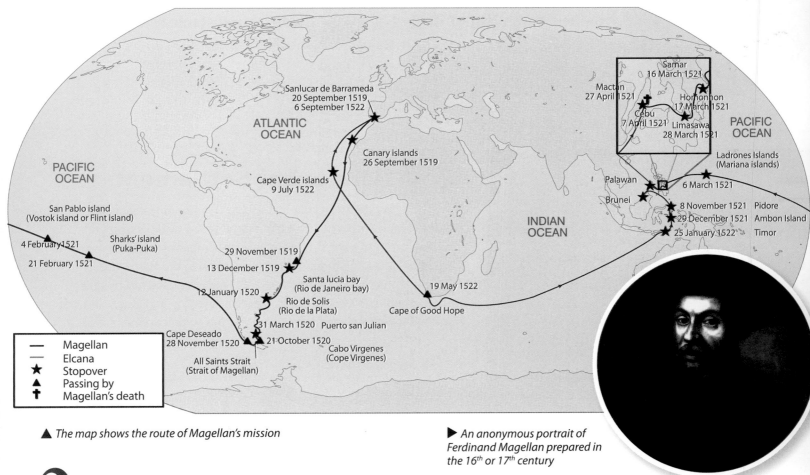

▲ *The map shows the route of Magellan's mission*

▶ *An anonymous portrait of Ferdinand Magellan prepared in the 16th or 17th century*

🔍 The Strait of Magellan

Like many explorers of his time, Magellan believed that one could sail to the Pacific Ocean through a shortcut across South America. On 20 September 1519, he left Spain with five ships: the *Trinidad*, *San Antonio*, *Concepcion*, *Santiago*, and *Victoria*.

Over the next year, they explored the waterways of Argentina, searching for a strait that cut across to the Pacific. On 21 October 1520, Magellan rounded the Cape of the Virgins. He entered the strait that would later bear his name. When he received news that the Pacific Ocean had been sighted, the iron-willed admiral broke down and cried with joy.

💡 Isn't It Amazing!

In 1966–1967, British adventurer Francis Charles Chichester completed the first solo circumnavigation of Earth. He was sailing the yacht, *Gipsy Moth IV*.

👤✓ In Real Life

About seven months into the journey, three of Magellan's ship captains mutinied. Magellan executed the captain of the *Victoria*. He then cut loose the *Concepcion's* anchor. As the ship drifted towards Magellan's own *Trinidad*, Captain Gaspar Quesada panicked and surrendered. The last captain, Juan de Cartagena of the *San Antonio*, also gave up.

Magellan **marooned** and executed some of the mutineers, but most were forgiven.

The Pacific Crossing

It was a parched, ill, and starving fleet that journeyed across the Pacific Ocean. The crews were surviving on rat-bitten biscuits and hard leather, but a determined Magellan kept them on course. After 99 days, they finally reached Guam and obtained fresh food. Magellan then steered towards the Philippines, where, in 1521, the catholic Raja Hamabon of Cebu became the first Pacific Island ruler to accept an alliance with Spain. Just weeks later, Magellan found himself in a battle on Mactan island. He was wounded by a bamboo spear, surrounded, and killed.

⊛ Incredible Individuals

Magellan was equal in skill to Vasco da Gama as a sailor, but many scholars tracking the history of Portugal overlook him as he sailed for the king of Spain. Historians from Spain overlook him as well, choosing to give credit to the discoveries of another navigator named Cano. However, Magellan's discoveries would not have been made without the patronage of the Spanish king.

◀ *Magellan's battle and death in the Philippines*

▼ *Shrine to Magellan at Mactan*

Proving Earth is Round

After Magellan's death, only two of his ships remained—the *Trinidad* and the *Victoria*. The *Trinidad* was no longer seaworthy. Cano, originally a member of the *Concepcion*, took charge of the *Victoria* and reached Spain on 8 September 1522. He thus conclusively showed that Earth was indeed a globe. Emperor Charles added on Cano's coat of arms the inscription '*Primus circumdedisti me*', which translated to 'You were the first to encircle me'.

A HERNANDO DE MAGALLANES

▲ *The Victoria was the only one of Magellan's five ships to circumnavigate the globe*

Exploring North America

English explorer Henry Hudson (1565–1611) is famous for his discoveries of the region around present-day New York. Hudson's journeys began as a search for an ice-free shortcut to Japan and China, by way of the North Pole. He set off in 1607 with his son John and ten others. On this voyage, he explored the polar ice front as far east as the Svalbard archipelago. He set out again on 22 April 1608, exploring the area between Svalbard and Novaya Zemlya islands, east of the Barents Sea. Unfortunately, he was forced to return after finding his path blocked by ice.

▲ *Aerial view of New York City and the Hudson River*

The Hudson River

In 1609, Hudson embarked on his third voyage on the ship *Half Moon*. While navigating the Atlantic shores, he encountered a vast river that had already been discovered in 1524 by Florentine navigator Giovanni da Verrazzano. However, this would eventually be called the Hudson River. By September, Hudson had passed Cape Cod, Chesapeake **Bay**, and Delaware Bay and reached the river's **estuary** without discovering any route to the Pacific.

▲ *A replica of the Dutch ship Halve Maen (Half Moon)*

▶ *Henry Hudson's statue in Henry Hudson Park*

Hudson Bay

Hudson's next journey led him to an inlet of water that would later be known as Hudson Strait. Sailing on the ship *Discovery* on 17 April 1610, Hudson stopped briefly in Iceland, then passed through the straits to Hudson Bay. Exploring it thoroughly, he landed in James Bay, the southern end of Hudson Bay, still finding no outlet to the Pacific.

Hudson eventually got stranded there for the winter. Quarrels arose among his people. On 22 June 1611, mutineers set Hudson and his son adrift on a small open boat. Neither of them were seen again. The ringleaders of the **mutiny** were themselves killed by Inuits before they reached home.

▲ *The Last Voyage of Henry Hudson, a painting by John Collier*

◀ *Henry Hudson entering New York bay on 11 September 1609, with a Native American family watching from the shore*

The Lands Down Under

Dutch navigator Abel Janszoon Tasman (1603–1659) was the first European to discover Tasmania, New Zealand, Tonga, and the Fiji Islands. For most of his life, Tasman was based in Batavia (now Jakarta), where he kept a lookout for rebels and smugglers. In 1642, Tasman was commissioned to explore the southern stretches of the Indian Ocean and map its lands.

Tasmania and New Zealand

On 16 August 1642, Tasman embarked with two ships—the *Heemskerk* and the *Zeehaen*—to Mauritius. Sailing south and east, he discovered new land on 24 November, which he named Van Diemen's Land (now Tasmania). On 13 December, Tasman and his crew became the first Europeans to sight New Zealand's South Island. They entered the strait between North and South Islands, exploring Murderers Bay, North Island's coasts, the Cook Strait, Cape Maria Van Diemen, and the Three Kings islands. They spent Christmas just east of Stephens and D'Urville islands.

In Real Life

This was the first time the Maori people of New Zealand saw Europeans. Tasman and seven crewmen tried to land on a small boat, but the Maori attacked them, killing three and leaving a fourth to die of wounds. Tasman thus named this area Murderers Bay.

◀ *A drawing by Isaack Gilsemans, Tasman's artist, illustrating the Dutch team surrounded by the Maori people at Murderers Bay (now Golden Bay), New Zealand*

Tonga and Fiji

Sailing northeast, Tasman discovered Tonga on 21 January and the Fiji Islands on 6 February. The ships then turned west and sailed back to Batavia through the New Guinea waters. The whole trip took 10 months and Tasman went around Australia without ever seeing it!

Australia

In 1644, Tasman embarked on a new expedition to search for a southern continent. This time, he steered southeast below New Guinea, through the Torres Strait and into Australia's Gulf of Carpentaria. Coasting along, Tasman was able to map the northern coast of Australia.

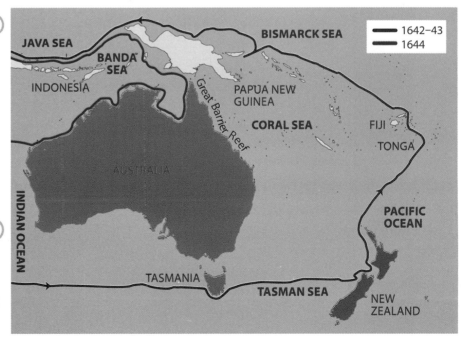

▲ *The map shows the route of Abel Tasman's first and second exploratory voyage around New Zealand and Australia. The first voyage was taken between 1642–43 and the second voyage was taken in 1644*

James Cook

Have you heard of James Cook (1728–1779)? He was a British navy captain famous for his explorations of Antarctica, Australia, and New Zealand in the south, and the Bering Strait and North America in the north. More amazingly, he set new benchmarks in seamanship, navigation, and map-making. He modernised attitudes regarding indigenous peoples and the care of sailors at sea. Cook peacefully changed the map of the world more than anyone else in history.

▲ *Official portrait of James Cook at the National Maritime Museum*

🔍 The Southern Hemisphere

In 1768, 40-year-old James Cook was made commander of a scientific expedition to the Pacific. Cook's job was to transport scientists of the Royal Society to Tahiti. And from there, to discover the mysterious southern continent, Terra Australis. Cook commanded HMS *Endeavour*, while the scientific mission itself was under the leadership of the wealthy 26-year-old scientist Joseph Banks.

◀ *Sir Joseph Banks (in the red coat), Captain James Cook (holding out his hat) with other British scientists and aristocrats*

▶ *A replica of HMS Endeavour at Cooktown Harbour, Australia*

🔍 Claiming Australia

For over six months in 1769, Cook thoroughly mapped New Zealand. Crossing west on the Tasman Sea, he arrived on Australia's southeast coast on 19 April 1770, becoming the first European to see this part of the continent. Cook named the area New South Wales and anchored at Botany Bay.

Exploring the 3,200 km area to the north from the coast, he even navigated the hazardous Great Barrier Reef, the Coral Sea, and the Torres Strait. On 22 August 1770, Cook claimed the eastern Australian coast for King George III and Britain.

▶ *On 14 February 1779, James Cook got into a fight with Hawaiians over a stolen boat. In the fracas, Cook was struck on the head and slain on the beach at Kealakekua*

💡 Isn't It Amazing!

Joseph Banks's mission was such a scientific success, it inspired other scientists to explore the world. Among them were Charles Darwin, Thomas Henry Huxley, and Joseph Dalton Hooker, whose voyages and works popularised the theory of evolution.

Measuring Antarctica

Over 1772–1775, Cook sailed out with two ships called the *Resolution* and the *Adventure*. He completed the first west-east circumnavigation near the Antarctic. He discovered New Caledonia in the Pacific, as well as the Atlantic's South Sandwich Islands and South Georgia island. Cook concluded that only the Terra Australis existed in Australia and New Zealand; the rest were frozen lands of Antarctica.

 ▶ On 11 June 1770, the Endeavour careened as she struck a coral spur. This part of the Great Barrier Reef has since been called the Endeavour Reef. Cook landed at the mouth of the Endeavour River in Queensland to repair the damages and set off again

▼ *Captain Cook's map of the southern hemisphere with the South Pole at the centre*

⊛ Incredible Individuals

Ships on long voyages used to have high death tolls owing to a disease called scurvy. This was essentially caused by a lack of Vitamin C, which was unknown in the 18th century. Cook lost none of his men to scurvy and only a few to fever and dysentery. This is because he was strict about cleanliness and ventilation in the sailors' quarters. He insisted that his team follow a diet of cress, sauerkraut, and orange extract, all high in Vitamin C. He thus became famous in naval circles for keeping his crew alive and healthy.

▼ *The Resolution and Adventure enter Matavai Bay, off the Pacific Ocean*

The Lewis and Clark Expedition

In 1803, the USA bought about 2,100,000 sq. km of land from Napoleon in the famous Louisiana Purchase. President Thomas Jefferson sent a mission to explore this new territory via the Missouri River. The expedition was led by his secretary Meriwether Lewis and Lewis's military superior William Clark.

🔍 An Epic Expedition

On 14 May 1804, they set off with four dozen people, and a dog named Seamen, from St. Louis. They sailed along the Missouri River on a 17 m keelboat and two smaller boats. The mission would eventually cover 13,000 km of pristine lands. At the time, they were populated by vast herds, abundant vegetation, and largely peaceful tribes. Over the next 2 years, 4 months, and 10 days, the **corps** would experience many adventures before returning to St. Louis on 23 September 1806.

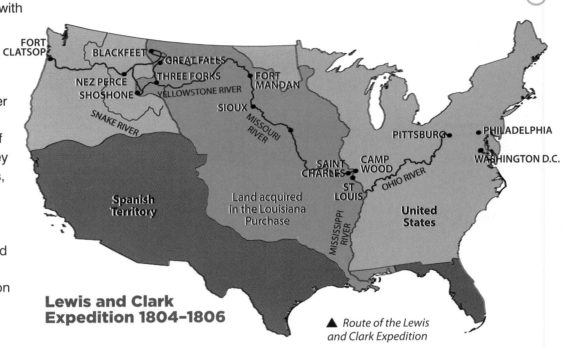

Lewis and Clark Expedition 1804-1806

▲ Route of the Lewis and Clark Expedition

▲ The Great Falls of Missouri River

▲ After leaving the Great Falls, the expedition came across extraordinary cliffs and named them Gates of the Rocky Mountains

🔍 Amazing Discoveries

They documented around 178 new plants, including *prairie sagebrush*, *Douglas fir*, and *ponderosa pine*. Plants were often named after the men, for instance, *Lewisia rediviva* (bitterroot), *Philadelphus lewisii* (mock orange), and *Clarkia pucella* (ragged robin). The grizzly bear, prairie dog, pronghorn antelope, and about 122 other animals were also found. The crew named new places after themselves, their loved ones, and even after their dogs—Seaman's Creek.

Diplomatic Successes

Lewis and Clark impressed the Native Americans, who were largely welcoming. In return for food, information, guides, and shelter, the expedition put on military parades, presented gifts, and offered greater trade and peace. There was even a 'magic show' with magnets, compasses, and an air gun. The expedition would leave cordially after issuing diplomatic invitations to Washington D.C.

Independence Day

In June 1805, Lewis reached a fork in the river. Taking the main south fork, he arrived at the Great Falls. The group had to carry their goods 29 km around the falls over broken, cacti-infested ground and past a number of grizzly bears. They completed the crossing on 4 July, in time to celebrate Independence Day by drinking and dancing the night away.

▲ In August 1805, Sacagawea's brother, the Shoshone tribe's Chief Cameahwait, helped the expedition purchase horses and find a path through the Rocky Mountains

◀ Passing through the Gates, they arrived at the beautiful Three Forks, where the Missouri meets the Jefferson (seen here), Gallantin, and Madison rivers

💡 Isn't It Amazing!

On 8 January 1806, Clark and Sacagawea found a whale skeleton on a beach. They bought **blubber** and oil from the Native Americans who were processing the whale.

Sacagawea, The Explorer

A member of the Shoshone tribe, Sacagawea joined the expedition as the wife of its member Toussaint Charbonneau. She was then 15 years old and pregnant. Sacagawea proved to be invaluable as an interpreter, negotiator, and a path-finder. She even showed the group how to find and cook local foods. Her calm and quick thinking saved the mission many times. When she eventually passed away, Clark adopted her two children Jean Baptiste and Lizette. Since 2000, the US treasury has minted a dollar coin named the Sacagawea Dollar in her honour.

◀ Sacagawea with her son Jean Baptiste, who was born during the expedition

▲ In July, Clark named a majestic rock outcrop Pompey's Tower (now, Pompey's Pillar) after Sacagawea's son, who was affectionately nicknamed Pomp. Clark also carved his own name and date on the Pillar

▲ Over July–August 1806, the crew explored Yellow River and the area around it. In another month, they would be home

The Evolution Revolution

At the age of 22, Englishman Charles Darwin (1809–1882) set sail on HMS *Beagle*. On the way, he spent many months exploring the islands and coasts around South America. Here, Darwin noticed strong patterns between life on the islands and on the main continent. For instance, he saw daisies and sunflowers as large as trees on one of the islands!

▶ *Charles Darwin waited more than 20 years to publish his theory on evolution*

🔍 Darwin's Findings

Darwin realised that plants and animals on the islands must have changed to take advantage of the homes they were provided. Thus, on an island that had no trees, the sunflowers evolved to become its trees. Darwin called this the 'theory of natural selection'. He realised that it made plants and animals successful at conquering new environments. This supported the groundbreaking idea that life was not created by God; instead, it evolved over thousands and thousands of years from interactions with nature.

◀ *A series of skulls show how human beings evolved from our ape-like ancestors*

◀ *The frigate bird lives near tropical oceans. Its wings evolved to take advantage of warm currents of air that rise upwards. The bird can thus soar without flapping its wings for hours and even days at a time*

👤 In Real Life

Genes are proteins in our bodies that decide whether we become a plant, a mouse, a human being, or something else. We inherit our genes from our ancestors. Did you know that 98 per cent of our genes are the same as a chimpanzee's? We share 92 per cent of our genes with mice. About half our genes are the same as a fly's. 18 per cent of our genes are the same as some weeds.

🔍 Voyage of the Beagle

On 27 December 1831, HMS *Beagle* set sail for South America. Her captain Robert Fitzroy was an aristocrat who feared being alone on the long voyage. So, he brought along Charles Darwin as a companion. Together, they faced five years of physical and mental hardships. They battled the seas, explored dense Brazilian jungles, and climbed inhospitable Andes mountains. By the end, Darwin had written a 770 page diary, with another 1,750 pages of notes. (He also had a collection of 5,436 skins, bones, and carcasses.) These were published as the famous book *The Voyage of the Beagle*.

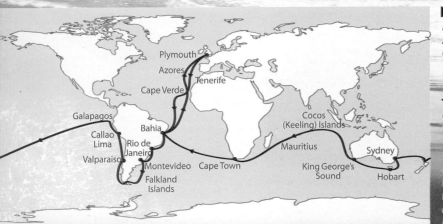

Plymouth
Azores
Tenerife
Cape Verde
Galapagos
Bahia
Callao
Lima
Rio de
Janeiro
Valparaiso
Montevideo
Cape Town
Falkland
Islands
Cocos
(Keeling) Islands
Mauritius
Sydney
King George's
Sound
Hobart

▶ *A painting of HMS Beagle in South America, by crewman Conrad Martens*

◀ *The Beagle set out from Plymouth, England, and made its way around South America to the Galapagos islands. From there, it crossed the Pacific, Indian, and Atlantic oceans to reach England again*

🔍 The Galapagos Archipelago

Darwin spent about five weeks on the islands of Galapagos, admiring and recording their extraordinary wildlife. Many of the creatures here are endemic, which means that they cannot be found anywhere else on Earth.

▶ *The giant Galapagos tortoise can live for up to 150 years. Darwin described them as antediluvian, meaning they were so old, they probably lived before Noah and the great flood*

◀ *Darwin came across a marine iguana for the first time. In amazement, he called them 'imps of darkness'*

🔍 Fossils

Darwin also discovered fossils of **extinct** animals in South America. Among them were the remains of giant sloths, mastodons, ancient armadillos, and animals that looked like rhinoceroses and horses. Darwin concluded that animals that could not adapt to changing environments would die out. Until he propounded his theory, people believed that the fossils found in South America were of mythical creatures destroyed by the gods in an ancient time.

▶ *The giant sloth of South America was the size of an elephant*

▲ *A Galapagos sea lion*

Discovering Africa

David Livingstone (1813–1873) was a Scottish missionary whose explorations of the African heartland gave Europeans their first look into the continent. Livingstone's first trip lasted 15 years. He spent this time travelling tirelessly across Africa, meeting its people, spreading his teachings, and condemning the abhorrent practice of slavery.

⊛ Incredible Individuals

During his 1844 trip, Livingstone courageously faced an attacking lion. His left arm was badly mauled. Eventually, he became unable to hold the barrel of his gun steadily. For the rest of his life, he was forced to fire from his left arm, and take aim using his left eye.

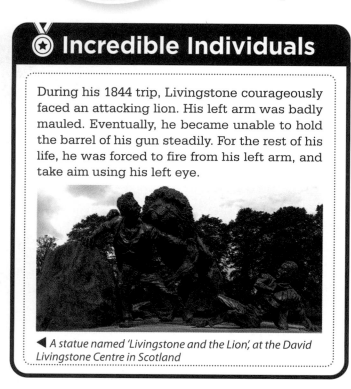

◀ *A statue named 'Livingstone and the Lion', at the David Livingstone Centre in Scotland*

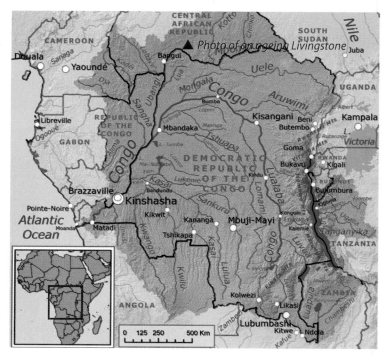

▲ *A map of Dr Livingstone's westernmost explorations in Africa*

🔍 The Hero of Victoria Falls

Between November 1853 and May 1854, Livingstone made an arduous journey to discover a path from Linyanti to the Atlantic coast. He then returned to Linyanti again and struck out east, exploring the Zambezi regions. On 16 November 1855, he came across a roaring, smoke-like waterfall on the Zambezi River. Claiming it for the British queen, he named it Victoria Falls. Livingstone returned to England and was received as a national hero.

▼ *On 1 August 1849, Livingstone and a small company became the first Europeans to sight Lake Ngami*

▶ *Victoria Falls, a UNESCO World Heritage Site at Mosi-oa-Tunya National Park, Zambia*

In Real Life

The Zambezi mission furthered British colonial influence in Africa. In 1893, this area became the British Central Africa Protectorate. In 1907, it became Nyasaland. Finally, in 1966, it became the Republic of Malawi.

▲ Lake Malawi, surrounded by forested hills

Rivers Zambezi and Ruvuma

Livingstone returned to Africa in 1858 and stayed till 1864. This time, he came with a party of Europeans with whom he further explored the Zambezi. On 17 September 1859, they became the first Britons to reach Ruvuma River. The mission helped amass a large and priceless body of scientific data.

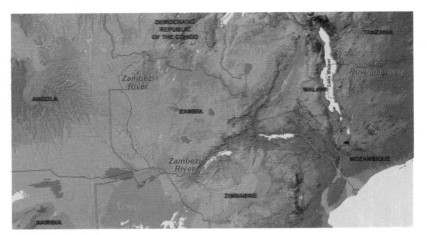

▲ The Zambezi River basin extends to Lake Malawi, which feeds the Ruvuma River

Farthest West

Livingstone was back in Africa by January 1866, exploring the area around Lake Tanganyika. At this time, his followers deserted him. They even cooked up stories about Livingstone's death. In the meantime, the man himself became the first European to reach Lake Mweru (1867) and Lake Bangweulu (1868). On 29 March 1871, he reached Nyangwe on the Lualaba River, the greatest source of the Congo River. This was farther west than any European had travelled within Africa.

▲ Lake Mweru

▲ Lake Bangweulu; the name translates as 'where water meets the sky'

At Rest in the South

Livingstone returned to Lake Tanganyika a sick man. Here, he was discovered by Henry M. Stanley, a reporter for the *New York Herald*. Stanley brought him much-needed medicine. Livingstone recovered, but refused to return home with Stanley. Instead, he journeyed south again. In May 1873, at Chitambo in northern Zambia, Africans found Livingstone dead by his bedside, kneeling as if in prayer. His body was taken back to England and buried with ceremony in Westminster Abbey.

In Real Life

Livingstone's geographical, technical, and medical discoveries are still being studied today. In spite of the prejudices of the time, Livingstone worked fervently for the emancipation of slaves and believed in Africa's potential as a modern state.

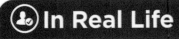

▲ Stanley in Africa, around the time he met Livingstone

◀ The illustration depicts the meeting of Stanley and Livingstone

Undercover Adventures

An English spy named Sir Richard Francis Burton (1821–1890) was the first European to see Lake Tanganyika in Africa and a number of Islamic cities that were forbidden to Westerners. Over his lifetime, he wrote 43 travel books. He also translated 30 books from other languages. Most famous among them is an amazing 16 volume edition of *The Arabian Nights*.

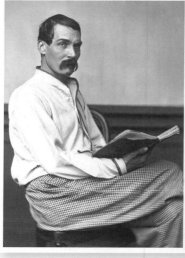

▲ *The young scholar and spy Richard Burton*

▲ *Demons, angels, murderers, and mythical beasts from Burton's translation of The Arabian Nights*

🔍 Mecca and Medina

In 1853, Burton dressed as a Pathan—an Afghan Muslim— and travelled to Cairo, Egypt. He made his way to Arabia to visit the sacred Medina. Following bandit-infested roads, Burton then travelled on to Mecca. At the time, no foreigners were allowed inside these two holiest of Islamic cities.

Facing a death sentence if he were caught, Burton snuck into the shrine of Ka'bah. He even sketched an accurate floor plan of this most sacred shrine of Islam. Burton published his journey as the *Pilgrimage to Al-Madinah and Mecca*. For the first time, people in the West saw the customs and manners of their Muslim contemporaries.

⭐ Incredible Individuals

Burton went to India in 1842 and became an intelligence officer—a spy! His job included visiting bazaars in disguise. There, he would secretly collect information from Muslim merchants. Over eight years, he mastered Arabic, Hindi, Marathi, Sindhi, Punjabi, Pashto, Telugu, and Multani. By the end of his life he knew 25 languages and 40 dialects!

◄ *The shrine at Mecca packed with people*

▶ *Richard Burton disguised as a Muslim man*

African Adventures

In 1854, Burton became the first European to enter the forbidden East African city of Harar, without being executed. In 1857–1858, he went hunting for the source of the Nile River. The leader of the expedition was John Speke. Although they failed to find the source, Speke pushed on northeast and discovered the magnificent Lake Victoria.

West Africa

In the 1860s, Burton was living in Fernando Po, an island near West Africa. During this time, he made frequent trips to the mainland and wrote five books about West African customs. These included fascinating discoveries about birth and death rituals, weddings, cannibalism, and ritual murders. Burton's writings made him very popular with scholars, but the government thought he was mad.

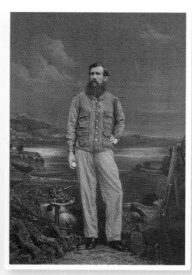

▲ *John Speke with Lake Victoria behind him*

Banishment and Books

Calling him dangerous, the government banished Burton far from his beloved Africa and India. Burton spent his time writing more books. In 1870, he published a translation titled *Vikram and the Vampire, or Tales of Hindu Devilry*. He also wrote a volume on the Sindh, two volumes on the gold mines of Midian, and a number of other titles. Burton risked imprisonment by translating many lovely books that were considered immoral by the rulers of Britain. Finally, in 1886, the government recognised the value of his life's work. In February 1886, he was knighted by Queen Victoria.

◄ *The fantastical artwork for Vikram and the Vampire, or Tales of Hindu Devilry were done by Ernest Griset*

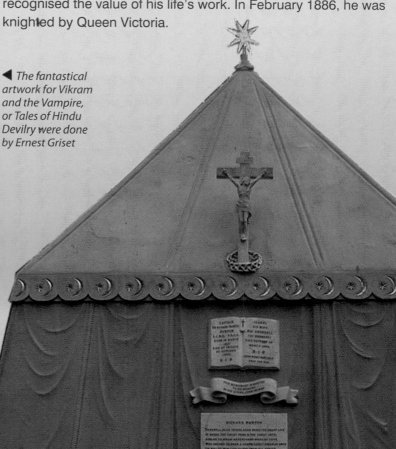

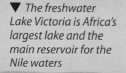

▼ *The freshwater Lake Victoria is Africa's largest lake and the main reservoir for the Nile waters*

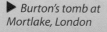

▶ *Burton's tomb at Mortlake, London*

Around the World in 72 Days

Nellie Bly (1864–1922) was the most accomplished female journalist of her time. She lived a life full of adventure, and became famous by beating the fictional record for time taken to travel around the world.

The Fearless Journalist

Elizabeth Cochrane—better known as Nellie Bly—wrote articles that were phenomenal and profound. She first wrote on the condition of working girls and slum life. In 1886–1887, she spent months in Mexico, reporting on government corruption. Her sharply critical articles angered Mexican officials and caused her expulsion from the country. In 1887, she faked insanity to get into an asylum and report about how the mentally ill were being mistreated. Bly made similar forays into factories, prisons, and even the legislature. Her work caught the attention of the public and brought about great social improvements. These important articles are now published as the books *Six Months in Mexico* and *Ten Days in a Madhouse*.

▼ Bly's trip made her so famous, there was a popular board game 'Round the World With Nellie Bly' named after her

Isn't It Amazing!

Bly's career began in 1885 when she sent an angry letter to the editor of the *Pittsburgh Dispatch*, against a mean-spirited article written about women. The editor was so impressed by her letter, he gave her a job as a reporter!

▶ Bly spent 6 months in Mexico writing about Mexican people before eventually upsetting the government

Racing Jules

In 1873, Jules Verne published his travel-adventure novel, *Around the World in Eighty Days*. In the story, fictional hero Phileas Fogg wins a bet by accomplishing the titular journey. In 1889, Nellie Bly was invited to beat this fictional record. Nearly a million people entered a guessing contest on how long she would take to complete the race. On 14 November, Bly sailed out of New York. She boarded ships, trains, rickshaws, **sampans**, horses, and **burros** all along her fantastic race. She finally returned to New York on a special train and was greeted by brass bands and fireworks. Her record was 72 days, 6 hours, 11 minutes, and 14 seconds.

▼ Bly's report on the Blackwell Island asylum's conditions caused a grand-jury investigation and led to improved standards in patient care

▶ Nellie Bly's reception at the end of her journey

The Lost Cities of the Incas

Machu Picchu is an ancient place high in the Andes mountains of South America. It was once home to the Incas. The ruins of Machu Picchu were discovered by German adventurer Augusto Berns in 1867. But the world did not hear about it until American archaeologist Hiram Bingham (1875–1956) began his explorations.

▶ The ruins of Machu Picchu, hidden in the Peruvian Andes, high above the Urubamba River valley

The Search for Machu Picchu

In July 1911, Bingham led a hunt for Vilcabamba, the 'lost city of the Incas'. Vilcabamba was their name for a 16th century mountain stronghold. Its location was a secret known only to the Incas. They used it to fight against Spanish conquerors. About 400 years later, the only clue to the city was a rumour, which said it was somewhere near Cuzco, in Peru.

At Cuzco, locals told Bingham to search the Urubamba River valley for the legendary site, Choquequirao, meaning 'Cradle of Gold'. Bingham had to trek 2,350 m up into the formidable Andes. On 24 July, the Quechua-speaking Melchor Arteaga led him to spectacular Incan ruins that lay in a saddle between the peaks Machu Picchu (Old Peak) and Huayna Picchu (New Peak).

▲ Melchor Arteaga crossing the Urubamba River, 24 July 1911

An Incan Fortress City

In 1912 and 1915, Bingham led expert teams to Machu Picchu. They realised that the site was a vast palace complex belonging to the ruler Pachacuti Inca Yupanqui, who ruled from 1438–1471. The city was built using thousands of stone-cut steps, high walls, mysterious tunnels, and other inventive structures!

▼ Remains of Incan buildings at Machu Picchu

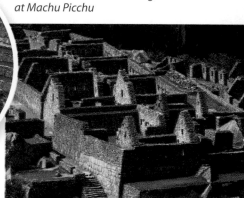

▼ Dry stone walls of the Temple of the Sun, Machu Picchu

▲ Giant stone terraces made farming possible on the steep mountainside

⊛ Incredible Individuals

Bingham's explorations also revealed the nearby sites of Vitcos and Espiritu Pampa. Gene Savoy, another American archaeologist, proved that Espiritu Pampa was in fact the real Vilcabamba. Over his lifetime, Savoy worked on more than 40 Incan and pre-Incan sites in Peru.

Cool Conquests

Roald Amundsen (1872–1928) was an explorer from Norway. He was the first person to reach the South Pole. He was also the first person to navigate a ship through the elusive Northwest Passage. Amundsen is one of the greatest figures in the history of polar exploration.

◄ *The stake on the right of the sign board marks the South Pole, while the board marks the achievements of explorers Roald Amundsen and Robert Scott*

🔍 The Northwest Passage

The Passage was a shortcut from the Atlantic Ocean to the Pacific Ocean by sailing across the Arctic region. People believed that such a route lay above the coasts of modern Canada. Yet its exact location was a mystery.

🔍 Amundsen's Way

In 1903, Roald Amundsen took up the challenge. His goal was to sail through the Northwest Passage and around the northern Canadian coast. After a long, hard journey, Amundsen was able to reach Cape Colborne in August 1905. By the following month he had completed the greater part of the passage. At this point, he was stopped by winter and ice. The crew was forced to stay at Herschel Island in the Yukon. Once the ice melted, they resumed their journey. Late in August 1906, they completed the route at Nome, Alaska. Amundsen was given a hero's welcome for his successful discovery of the passage!

💡 Isn't It Amazing!

Explorers had been searching for the Northwest Passage for centuries! As far back as 1497, King Henry VII of England sent John Cabot in search of a northwest passage to eastern Asia. His explorations led to British claims over Canada.

▲ *A depiction of John Cabot departing Bristol to explore the Americas*

◄ *To conquer the Northwest Passage, Amundsen sailed out with six men on a 42,637 kg sloop named Gjöa*

▲ *Christmas dinner for the Gjöa crew, 1903*

◄ *Amundsen and his crew aboard the Gjöa at the end of the trip at Nome, Alaska on 1 September 1906*

South Pole

In June 1910, Amundsen headed for the South Pole. Sailing the Fram Strait, he reached the Bay of Whale in Antarctica and set up a base camp. Experienced in the ways of ice and snow, Amundsen carefully prepared for the journey. He knew that accidents were common on polar lands. So, he made a trip halfway to the pole, to store emergency food supplies all along the way. He used sled dogs to transport his supplies.

▲ The crew sewing polar kits in the living room of the Fram

▲ One of the food deposits; Amundsen laid down about 2,721 kg of supplies, equipment, and fuel

▲ On the way to the South Pole

The Historic Trip

On 19 October 1911, Amundsen set out with four men, four sledges, and 52 dogs. The weather was on their side for the next couple of months. The group reached the South Pole on 14 December. The explorers stayed there until the 17th, making scientific observations. They safely returned to the Bay of Whales on 25 January 1912.

▲ Roald Amundsen, Helmer Hanssen, Sverre Hassel, and Oscar Wisting at the South Pole on 17 December 1911

▼ Robert Scott's team at the South Pole

⊛ Incredible Individuals

A rival team of explorers was chasing the South Pole at the same time as Amundsen. It was led by the English explorer Robert Scott. This group's base camp was 100 km farther from the pole than Amundsen's. Also, they used ponies instead of sled dogs for transport. Scott's team arrived at the South Pole on 17 January 1913—one month after Amundsen. Tragically, Scott's team faced bad weather, ran out of food and fuel, and died in Antarctica.

The Race to the North Pole

The geographical North Pole is found at a latitude of 90° N. This is a point at which all the globe's longitudes come together. The ocean around it is covered with ice. The first person to try to reach the North Pole was Henry Hudson in 1607.

🔍 Early Polar Records

Almost 160 years later, the second attempt was made by a Russian named Vasily Yakovlevich Chichagov. He reached just north of 80° latitude. Barriers of ice forced him to turn back! Over 1771–1871, many explorers made a push for the pole, but none succeeded. In 1871, American Charles Francis Hall got as close as 82° N. Tragically, Hall passed away that winter, soon after his ship *Polaris* got stranded in ice.

◀ *The funeral of Captain Charles Francis Hall*

🔍 The Fram Revelation

In 1893, a crew led by Norwegian explorer Fridtjof Nansen sailed towards the pole. They were on the *Fram*, a ship specially designed to avoid getting crushed by ice. Nansen's idea was to intentionally sail into an ice pack! When this happened, the design of the ship raised it above the ice. The ship then drifted polewards for almost three years. A great deal of scientific information was collected at this time. Most importantly, people realised that the way to the North Pole was not via open sea; rather it was covered in ice. One could not simply get there by ship.

◀ *The Fram braving the Arctic ice*

🔍 The Fram Expedition's Record

Just by drifting, the *Fram* reached 84° N in 1896. At this point, Nansen and his crewman Hjalmar Johansen set off over the solid ice of Franz Josef Land on a sledge. They reached just beyond 86° N before winter set in and worsening conditions forced them to return.

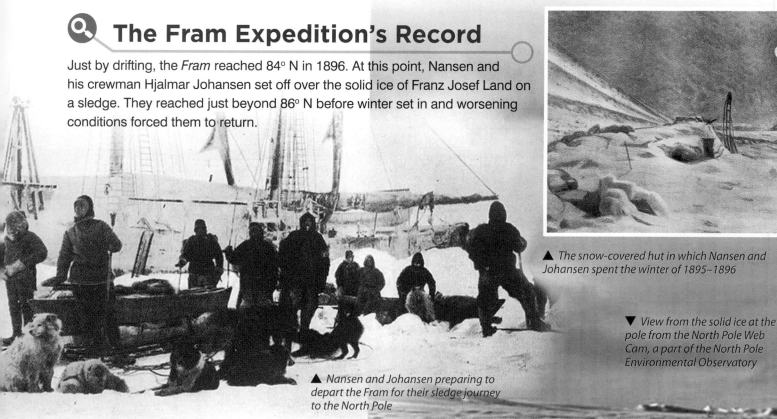

▲ *The snow-covered hut in which Nansen and Johansen spent the winter of 1895–1896*

▼ *View from the solid ice at the pole from the North Pole Web Cam, a part of the North Pole Environmental Observatory*

▲ *Nansen and Johansen preparing to depart the Fram for their sledge journey to the North Pole*

Controversial Claims

With the information from the *Fram*, a great race began. Explorers vied to be the first to reach the North Pole. In 1909, American Robert Peary claimed he had reached the pole from Cape Columbia. Just before Peary's return, another American named Fredrick A. Cook announced that he had reached the pole from Axel Heiberg Island, with the help of Inuits. However, neither of them could show proof of their claims. Both men's achievements are surrounded by doubt, even today.

▶ *Peary's team at what they claimed was the North Pole*

▲ *USS Skate surfacing in the Arctic, 1959*

Confirmed Records

On 12 May 1926, Roald Amundsen set off from Spitsbergen in an airship and flew across the pole to Alaska. Along with him were Lincoln Ellsworth and Umberto Nobile. These are the first known people to have reached and crossed the North Pole. In 1958, the US nuclear submarine *Nautilus* reached the pole under water. The next year, nuclear submarine *Skate* reached the pole and surfaced. In 1968, an American team led by Ralph Plaisted visited the pole by snowmobile. In 1977, the powerful Soviet icebreaker ship *Arktika* sailed all the way to the pole from the New Siberian Islands.

▲ *Norge, the semi-rigid airship that flew Amundsen and team over the North Pole*

▼ *Russian Ivan Papanin, leader of the first expedition to set up an ice station at the North Pole, 1937*

◀ *The Russian nuclear icebreaker Arktika*

On Top of the World

▲ *In Nepal, Everest is called Sagarmatha. It lies in the UNESCO World Heritage Site of Sagarmatha National Park, a 1,234 sq. km area that was set up in 1976*

The world's highest mountain above sea level is Mount Everest. It is 8,850 m high and is located in the Himalayas on the borders of Nepal and Tibet. The first people to reach its summit were New Zealand mountain climber Edmund Hillary (1919–2008) and Tibetan mountaineer Tenzing Norgay (1914–1986).

◀ *Vibrant fauna from around Sagarmatha, such as the blood pheasant (left) and the Himalayan monal (right)*

The First Expeditions

No human being lives on Everest. However, its valleys are home to Tibetan communities, like the Sherpas. They used to avoid climbing the high peaks, believing that gods and demons lived there. The first group to explore the area around Everest was a British team in 1921. In 1924, another team climbed as high as 8,546 m. Until WWII began in 1939, many teams came to conquer Everest, but failed. However, they explored and mapped routes that made it possible for future teams to succeed.

In Real Life

Since Hillary and Norgay's 1953 climb, more than 7,600 people have reached the peak of Everest. Tragically, some 300 mountaineers have died in the attempt.

◀ *Tenzing Norgay first attempted scaling Everest as part of a 1935 team when he was only 19 years old. Over the next few years, he took part in more Everest expeditions than anyone else*

▲ *In 1950, China took over Tibet and closed the northern route to Everest. In 1951, Nepal gave people permission to climb the mountain from its land*

Isn't It Amazing!

If you measure a mountain from its foot to its peak, the tallest mountain in the world is Mauna Kea in Hawaii. It is 10,205 m high. The part that you see is only 4,205 m high. The rest of it lies under water!

▶ *The volcanic Mauna Kea, Hawaii*

The Steps to the Summit

On the Northeast Ridge of Everest, there are three formidable 'steps' just before the summit. These steps are steep rock faces that make it difficult to reach the peak. The First Step is a straight limestone wall about 34 m high. Above it is a ledge. The Second Step begins here and is 50 m high. In 1975, the Chinese actually fixed a ladder over it, to make the climb easier! The Third Step is sheer rock-face about 30 m high. It leads to a slope that rises to the summit.

▶ *A mountaineer skiing down the steep Northeast Ridge*

The Ascent of 1953

A British team led by Colonel John Hunt and Baron Hunt set out for Everest in 1953. On 28 May, they set up a camp for the night at 8,500 m. Hillary and Norgay set out for the summit early next morning. After hours of brutal trekking, they reached the peak of Everest at 11:30 am. The men shook hands and hugged each other. Hillary took photos and left a crucifix. Tenzing, a Buddhist, made offerings to the mountain. The two men ate some sweets and spent about 15 minutes on top of the world. By 2 June, the entire team was back at the base camp. The joyous news broke out in London on the same day that Queen Elizabeth II was crowned! Edmund Hillary wrote about his journey in *High Adventure* (1955). He came back to the Everest region many times in the early 1960s, but never again climbed the peak. *Time Magazine* named him and Tenzing Norgay among the 100 most influential people of the 20th century.

▲ *The first photos of Everest from an airplane were taken in 1933*

1st **2nd** **3rd**

▶ *The north face of the Everest showing the location of the Three Steps*

◀ *The two photographs show Tenzing Norgay and Edmund Hillary during and after their historical climb*

ELECTRONICS & COMMUNICATIONS

BREAKTHROUGHS IN ELECTRONICS AND COMMUNICATION

Can you imagine your life in the absence of modern-day labour-saving gizmos and tech-powered entertainment? Amazingly though, electronics have been around for just over 100 years. This is no more than a blip in the long, long timeline of human existence.

Great leaps in technology—particularly in communications—were made during the many wars of the previous century. In fact, you would be surprised by just how much scientists, spies, and undercover agents have in common! Our treasured gadgets may have started out as a means for sending secret codes across oceans, or as pure scientific curiosity, but they have now taken over our homes, schools, and workplaces. So, what are the important inventions that have become indispensable to us? Read on to find out!

▼ *Budding scientists tinkering with robots*

Vacuum Tubes

Did you know that you could create electricity by heating certain materials? Thomas Edison (1847–1931) first observed this in 1875, when he was fiddling around with a light bulb. A few years later, British engineer John Ambrose Fleming (1849–1945) used his discovery to invent the first **vacuum tube**, called a diode.

After the diode, vacuum tubes became more complex. Until a few decades ago, they were used to power lots of communication devices. This included radios, televisions, and even computers.

▲ *Fleming's device began the age of electronics*

 ## How Does it Work?

Electricity is generated when lots of tiny, invisible particles called **electrons** travel across a medium. A stream of moving electrons is called an electric current. The vacuum tube behaves like an electric switch. When you turn it on, electricity runs through it. The tube looks like a glass bulb. Inside it, is a plate called the **anode**, and a filament called the **cathode**. Air is removed from the bulb, creating a **vacuum**.

If you send electricity into the cathode, it will become glowing hot and give off electrons. These electrons travel through the vacuum to the anode, creating an electric current. If you stop heating the cathode, it will stop releasing electrons, and the current will be 'switched off'.

▼ *A vacuum tube with a glowing cathode filament*

Modern Uses of Vacuum Tubes

Vacuum-tube technology is rarely used in the 21st century, as it has become obsolete. Nevertheless, there are a handful of applications for this gadget. Vacuum tubes are used in high-quality stereo systems. These stereo systems are used by music professionals and sound technicians.

Vacuum tubes are also used in instruments such as electric guitars. They have vacuum-tube amplifiers. Similarly, fluorescent displays are often thin vacuum-tube displays used to convey simple information in audio and video equipment. X-ray machines, radars, and even microwave ovens sometimes are fitted with vacuum tubes.

▲ *A modern sound amplifier with vacuum tubes*

⊛ Incredible Individuals

J.J. Thomson (1856–1940) was the son of an English bookseller. He revolutionised the world of physics by discovering the electron. For this, he received a Nobel Prize in 1906 and was knighted by King Edward VII in 1908.

Semiconductors and Microchips

Vacuum tubes were known to be bulky and breakable. Thus, early electronic machines took up a lot of space and needed frequent repair. During 1947–1948, three Americans—John Bardeen, Walter Brattain, and William Shockley—invented the **transistor**, which replaced vacuum tubes in electronics. This is because the transistor was small and sturdy, required very little power, and released very little heat.

Semiconductors

A transistor is made primarily of silicon, a substance found in sand and glass. Silicon is a **semiconductor**. This means that the way it conducts electricity can be changed by adding other materials to it.

▶ A microchip may include as many as 30 layers of complex circuitry

Microchips

The first transistors were used to make lighter machines, like portable radios and hearing aids. During the 1960s and 70s, scientists began to draw tiny electric circuits on to silicon chips. This created Integrated Circuits (IC), also called **microchips**. These circuits acted like wires to conduct electricity.

These days, a single microchip—which is smaller than the tip of your finger—can hold thousands of transistors. They are used to make everything, from toasters and phones to super computers and robots.

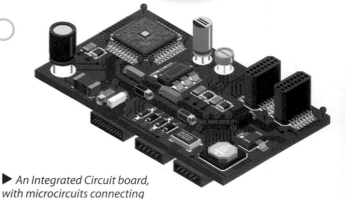

▶ An Integrated Circuit board, with microcircuits connecting different parts of the board

In Real Life

The first proper digital computer, Electronic Numerical Integrator and Computer (ENIAC), was built during World War II. It weighed 30,000 kg, used 18,000 vacuum tubes and gave off a lot of heat! This massive machine occupied an entire basement, where it was arranged in the shape of the letter U along three walls.

◀ Experts operating the gargantuan ENIAC, 1946

Batteries

A battery stores electrical energy in chemical form. In the year 1800, Italian physicist Alessandro Volta (1745–1827) invented the first modern battery. Volta arranged zinc and copper plates in a pile, like a stack of coins. In between the plates, he placed pieces of vinegar- or brine-soaked leather, or pasteboard. This was the first structure that allowed scientists to store and use electricity in a controlled manner.

Volta's battery is called the voltaic cell. Today, there are many varieties of batteries. Some are single-use or primary batteries, while others are rechargeable or secondary batteries.

▲ *A voltaic cell is sometimes called a galvanic cell*

▲ *Lithium ion batteries have an average of 600 charge cycles*

Commonly-used Batteries

Lithium-ion batteries are so light and small, they are called cells. They are rechargeable, long-lasting, environment-friendly, and used in phones and computers. You can even use solar power, that is, the sun's energy, to recharge these cells.

Big rectangular lead-acid batteries are fitted into car engines. They are used to start the car and power its air-conditioner, radio, GPS, and other devices. These batteries last up to four years on an average.

AA and AAA batteries are most commonly used in remote controls, headphones, clocks, and portable players. The AA batteries are slightly larger and stronger than the AAA batteries.

Most of our watches run on small alkaline batteries that are cost-effective and easily available. However, expensive watches use cells that contain lithium or silver oxide, which are much more reliable.

Disposing Used Batteries

Many batteries contain toxic chemicals that can leak out and affect you and your surroundings. Lead and cadmium, for instance, can stunt growth, lower the IQ, cause breathing and digestion problems and even cancer. So, deposit the used batteries at a recycling unit, where experts can safely get rid of harmful chemicals.

▶ *Used batteries should not be chucked away like regular dry garbage*

Calculators

The first calculators were mechanical, not electrical. They were simple wooden frames with rows of beads, representing 10s, 100s, and 1,000s. This invention was called an abacus and was used as far back as in 2,000 BCE in ancient Egypt.

In the 17th century, a new type of calculator called the slide rule was invented. This contained different scales that could slide against each other to do multiplications, divisions, and other arithmetic calculations. For the next 300 years, this was the most popular calculator in use. In the 19th century, inventors continued to make mechanical calculating machines that became smaller and easier to use.

▲ *The person who uses the abacus is called an abacist*

Electrical Calculators

Today's digital calculators are based on a machine called the 'arithmometer', invented by French mathematician Blaise Pascal (1623–1662) in 1642. In the mid 1950s, electronic data processing gave rise to the first electronic calculators. By the late 20th century, they could perform arithmetic that most mathematicians could not solve using pen and paper.

Nowadays, calculators have memory space and are programmable like computers. Indeed, most calculators come inbuilt into your phone and computer.

▲ *Arithmometers sat on your desk like old typewriters*

◄ *Modern calculators come with keys for unique arithmetic functions. Some are so sophisticated, they are powered by solar cells*

◄ *The Curta Calculator, 1948*

Incredible Individuals

The first portable calculator was also a mechanical device. It was invented by Austrian engineer Curt Herzstark during World War II. Herzstark was arrested by the Nazis for being Jewish. He was sent to the Buchenwald Concentration Camp. However, he was so knowledgeable and skilled, the Nazis spared his life, but continued to exploit his intellect.

Solar Energy

Do you know the meaning of the word 'photovoltaic'?
It refers to converting light into electrical energy. Sunlight or solar energy can thus be turned into electricity. This is an amazing alternative to other forms of energy, as it reduces pollution and is renewable.

Solar Cells

The sun's energy is converted into electrical energy by small devices called solar cells. Thousands of cells are arrayed to form panels. Large groups of panels are then used as power stations. They distribute electricity to factories, offices, and homes. People can even install solar panels on their rooftops to harness solar energy for their homes.

Renewable, Clean Energy

Conventional energy sources, such as wood, coal, petrol, and nuclear materials leave toxic waste every time they are used. In comparison, solar energy is clean, as it generates no refuse and does not harm your health or the environment. There is also an endless supply of this energy.

1954

Darryl Chapin, Calvin Fuller, and Gerald Pearson patent a way of using silicon in solar cells.

1905

Albert Einstein publishes his paper on the photoelectric effect and the theory of relativity. He wins the Nobel Prize for his findings, in 1921.

▲ *A solar eclipse helped make Einstein and his theory of general relativity world famous*

1839

Alexandre-Edmond Becquerel discovers the photovoltaic effect.

1860–90s

French mathematician August Mouchet and his assistant, Abel Pifre, construct the first solar-powered engines.

1891

American inventor Clarence Kemp patents the first commercial solar water heater.

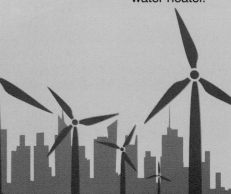

▲ *Alexandre Becquerel*

The Solar Timeline

1955

Solar cells begin to be made for commercial use. Early products include money-changers and devices that decode computers of the era.

Mid-1950s

Architect Frank Bridgers designs the first office building that uses solar water heating.

◀ *Solar panels on a satellite*

1958

Vanguard I becomes the first space satellite to use a solar array to power its radios. In the same year, Explorer III, Vanguard II and Sputnik 3 are all launched with solar-powered systems. Even today, this is the accepted energy source for space applications.

1981

Paul MacCready flies the first solar-powered aircraft called the Solar Challenger from France to England. The Challenger has over 16,000 solar cells on its wings.

1963

Japan installs a 242-W, photovoltaic array on a lighthouse.

1982

Hans Tholstrup drives the Quiet Achiever— the first solar-powered car—between Sydney and Perth in Australia. It proves to be far more efficient than the first gasoline-powered car.

▲ *Recharge station of a solar-powered car*

2000

Astronauts begin installing solar panels on the International Space Station in the largest array ever seen in space. There are 32,800 cells in each 'wing' of the array.

▲ *The International Space Station has four solar arrays*

1983

The first stand-alone home to be powered by solar cells is built in the Hudson River Valley, USA.

▲ *Solar panels are the fastest energy source to set up*

Telegraph

The telegraph was the first electric as well as the first wireless technology that allowed us to send long-distance messages quickly. In the early 1800s, electricity was still new. At this time, two Germans—Carl Gauss (1777–1855) and Wilhelm Weber (1804–1891)—built the first real electric telegraph. However, this machine could not send messages beyond 1 kilometre. During this period, other inventors came up with their own versions of the telegraph, but none of them really took off.

▲ An illustration of an old telegraph office (1867)

Samuel Morse and the Code

In the 1830s, American inventor Samuel F. B. Morse (1791–1872) invented a system of dots and dashes to match the English alphabet. This system, called the Morse Code, made it easy to telegraph messages on a new model that he developed. In 1843, Morse was asked by the American government to build a 60-km-long telegraph system. Public use of this first telegraph line began on 24 May 1844, with Morse sending the message, 'What hath God wrought!' By 1851, the USA had over 50 telegraph companies.

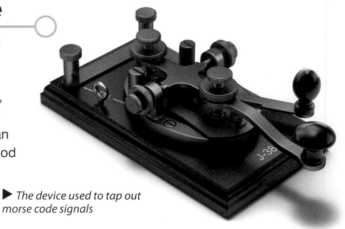

▶ The device used to tap out morse code signals

Radio Waves and the Wireless Telegraph

In 1888, a German physicist named Heinrich Hertz (1857–1894) discovered that it was possible to transmit electrical energy through the air. This energy travelled in invisible waves and eventually came to be called **radio waves**.

Over 1894–1896, Italian scientist Guglielmo Marconi (1874–1937) experimented with various ways of sending signals in Morse Code using radio waves. By 1906, he had refined his system so well that he was able to send messages across the Atlantic Ocean. He is thus the inventor of the wireless telegraph.

◀ A telegraph operator sending messages by tapping them out in Morse code

▼ A stamp featuring Guglielmo Marconi, who won the Nobel Prize for Physics in 1909. His discoveries in wireless communication are the basis for our modern understanding of long-distance radio

Radio

In the early 1900s, Canadian engineer Reginald Fessenden (1866–1932) was able to combine sound from a microphone with a type of electromagnetic wave to send messages over long distances. These electromagnetic waves are now called radio waves and are used by many devices other than the radio, including TV and mobile phones.

Fessenden made the first ever public radio broadcast in America on the eve of Christmas in 1904. He played 'O Holy Night' on his violin and could be heard by ships that were 160 km away. However, regular public broadcasting only began in 1920.

⊚ Incredible Individuals

In 1938, Orson Welles (1915–1985) rewrote *The War of the Worlds*—a book about Martians invading Earth—as a radio drama. Broadcasted as a Halloween special, the drama began with a series of fake news bulletins. The bulletins lasted an hour and seemed so real that many people believed they were truly being attacked by aliens. Entire cities became hysterical and were thrown into a turmoil!

▲ *Reginald Fessenden, the inventor of the radio, a photo from c. 1906*

🔍 The Early Days of Radio

All radio systems since then have worked using a transmitter that sends sound signals, and a receiver, which finds the signal and lets us hear radio programmes. Nowadays, radio broadcasting happens over two main types of channels: **AM** and **FM**.

AM channels can be heard over thousands of miles and are usually used to broadcast news, sports, and talk shows. FM channels offer better sound quality and are more popular. They travel shorter distances and are used by local police, taxis, and other groups to listen to information, music, and entertainment shows.

Surprisingly, when you listen to a live concert on the radio, the music reaches you faster than it does a person in the actual concert hall. This is because your radio transmits sound to you in the form of electric signals at the speed of light. In contrast, sound waves—the vibrations made by a voice or instrument—travel more slowly through the air to reach the person in the hall.

▲ *An electronic survey system of radio transmitters and monitors*

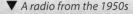

▼ *A radio from the 1950s*

👆 In Real Life

If you have an AM radio, you can use the radio and a nine-volt battery with a coin to create radio waves! Switch on the radio and turn the dial till you hear static—steady crackling noises. While holding the battery near the radio's antenna, quickly tap the two terminals on the battery with a coin, so they are connected for an instant. Try this fun trick and you will be able to hear the radio waves.

▶ *A 9 volt battery*

Television: Moving Pictures Sent on Radio Waves

All TVs need three things to function. These are the TV camera, which turns sound and picture into a signal; the TV transmitter, which sends the signal using radio waves; and the TV set at home or the receiver, which turns the signal back into image and sound.

Broadcasting and Cable

The earliest TV broadcasts were seen—mostly by scientists—in the late 1920s. But by the 1950s, there was steady public interest in TV shows. Cable TV was invented around this time and it streamed many more channels than regular radio transmission. It took around 30 years for cable TV to be accepted around the world! These days, TVs use satellite dishes as transmitters and receivers to provide high-definition, high-quality programmes.

▼ *A film strip showing a sequence of still shots from the Trinity Test, the first nuclear explosion conducted by humans*

In Real Life

The first TVs could only stream black-and-white content. Much later, engineers discovered that any colour can be made by mixing the three primary colours: red, green, and blue. Eventually, inventors made cameras that could capture separate red, green, and blue signals; transmission systems that could beam colour signals; and TV sets that could turn them into multicoloured images.

▶ *The first TVs had tiny screens and showed only black-and-white images*

Some Brilliant Minds behind the TV

In the 1880s, people were thinking, if voices can be sent over the air, why not pictures? In 1884, German inventor Paul Nipkow (1860–1940) used spinning discs with small holes in them to break up images into smaller elements. He was then able to recombine these into a black-and-white image. In 1906, Boris Rosing (1869–1933) of Russia combined Nipkow's disc with the Cathode Ray Tube (CRT) to develop the first basic TV set. In 1931, the spinning disc was once and for all replaced by the electronic camera, invented by another Russian, Vladimir Zworykin (1888–1982).

◀ *John Logie Baird with his television receiver; he invented the first publicly demonstrated colour television system*

Flat Screen TVs and 3D Technology

With the invention of LCD, plasma screen, and OLED technologies, TVs became as flat as the walls they are mounted on. LCD and plasma TVs have millions of tiny picture elements called pixels, which give us sharp images. OLED TVs use electricity to generate light particles called **photons** to display even better images.

Nowadays, engineers are trying to bring images out of the screen and into 'real' space. You may have seen this in movie halls when you're given glasses to watch 3D movies. There is still a long way to go for this technology with many exciting inventions to come.

◀ *3D and 4K televisions are becoming popular today*

⊙ Incredible Individuals

On 26 January 1926, Scottish inventor John Logie Baird (1888–1946) gave the world its first experience of true television. Only 50 scientists saw it, however, in an attic in London!

Baird formed the first TV studio—the Baird Television Development Company. In 1928, the BTDC sent TV signals across the Atlantic Ocean all the way to New York, and even to ships in the middle of the ocean. Baird also gave the world's first demonstration of colour television.

Who Invented the Telephone?

Most people think that the telephone was invented by Alexander Graham Bell (1847–1922) in 1876. But nobody knows the amazing story behind the real inventor! In 1841, Italian inventor Antonio Meucci (1808–1889) had already designed a telephone. He applied to the government for recognition in 1871. But the officials stalled and ignored him.

◄ Bell's first telephone was called the Centennial Model because it was first seen by the public on 25 June 1876 at the Centennial Exhibition in Philadelphia, USA

▼ An old battery operated phone

▲ A wooden telephone from the late 19ᵗʰ century

► Early tall telephones were called candlesticks

🔍 Isn't It Amazing!

The first words Bell ever spoke over the telephone were to his assistant. He said, 'Mr. Watson, come here. I want to see you.'

The Full Story

Bell shared a lab with Meucci in 1870s. In 1876, Bell wrote to the government about the invention of telephone. It was a similar invention for which Meucci has earlier applied for but was ignored. This time, the officials responded, and he became rich and famous! A furious Meucci sued Bell for fraud. But Meucci was an old man by then. He died before he could win the case. In 2002, well over a century later, the US Congress acknowledged Meucci's contributions.

American professor Elisha Gray (1835–1901) also developed a telephone. It is suggested that he filed for government recognition on the same day as Alexander Graham Bell! The date was 14 February 1876. Records show that Bell was the fifth person to file a notice that day. Gray was the 39th. Rather than investigate Gray's claims, the Patent Office simply named Bell the inventor of the telephone.

▲ *Elisha Gray also invented a musical telegraph*

Battery-operated Phones

Early phones did not rely on the phone company for electricity. They had a built-in magneto, which used a coil and a magnet-generated electric current. To use these phones, you first "recharged" the battery by cranking up a lever on its right side. If you did not do this, the phone at the other end would not ring.

◀ *The first cordless phone was invented in 1962 for the World Fair in Seattle, USA*

⊙ Incredible Individuals

The first phone book suggested a cheery 'hulloa' as a greeting. Bell thought 'Ahoy' was a better option. It was Thomas Edison who made 'Hello' the standard phone greeting.

To end the call, the phone book suggested 'God be with you', which got shortened to 'goodbye' and 'bye-bye'.

▼ *Candlestick phones soon gave way to rotatory-dial and push-button telephones*

Cell Phones:
Old Technology for a Modern Invention

Do you know how cell phones work? They use batteries and radio waves. When you make a call, your phone uses FM radio waves to signal the nearest antenna tower. The tower then sends your signal forward to a central tower, which in turn connects you to the landline or cell phone you are calling.

In most places, a tower can receive signals from around 25–26 sq. km. This area is called a cell; and this is why your phone is called a cell phone. As you travel, towers from different cells forward the signal.

🔍 SIM Card

If you open the back of your phone, you will see that it holds a battery and a shiny small card. This is called the SIM card. It became a part of cell phones in the early 1990s. The SIM is a microchip that holds all your identification and security details. Even if your phone gets damaged, you can put this chip into another phone and get back some of your contacts and text messages. The smallest SIM card in use today is called a Nano-SIM.

▲ SIM is short for Subscriber Identity Module

▲ The microchip of a SIM card is made of silicon along with other metals including phosphorus and gold

Smartphones

The first semblance of smartphones came out in the 1990s. These were the IBM Simon and the Nokia Communicator 9000. The first real smartphone came out in 2,000—the Ericsson R380. It was followed by phones like the Palm and BlackBerry, which were hugely successful. In 2007, Apple revolutionised smartphones by releasing the iPhone. This technology has been popular ever since.

◀ *Ericsson R380, Nokia Communicator, and a Blackberry phone*

Operating Systems

Smartphones these days are as smart as computers. So they need an Operating System (OS) to do their work. The three major OSs used in smartphones are Android by Google, iOS by Apple and Windows by Microsoft. Just because two phones run the same OS doesn't mean the phones are the same. There are physical differences between them such as weight and screen size. The speed of the phone and its memory can also vary. Furthermore, there may be differences in software, as manufacturers load different programmes and apps on to the phones.

▲ *These logos represent the three giants of the smartphone industry, Microsoft, Android, and Apple*

In Real Life

Our smartphones are now so capable and well-connected, they can interact with reality. For instance, apps can use data from satellites in the sky to tell us about our surroundings in real time. You can simply point your phone at the road ahead of you, and the app will show you bits of information about it, along with the route ahead. You can find fun new places and even play games like Pokemon Go with such augmented reality.

▶ *Steve Jobs—the founder of Apple—introduced the first iPhone on 9 January 2007*

Indispensable Office Technology

A photocopier is a machine that can reproduce text or images on paper by using light, heat, chemicals, and electricity. The first of its kind was developed in America in 1937 by the physicist Chester Carlson (1906–1968). Most modern offices use photocopiers. These are also called Xerox machines, after the most commonly known photocopier brand.

Inside the machine is a light-sensitive surface covered with ink or toner. When light passes through the paper that is being copied, the ink is sprayed on another sheet, forming a copy of the original. Electric charges are used on the ink and the copy paper to ensure the ink sticks to the new sheet. Finally, heat is applied to fuse the ink on to the paper.

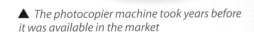

▲ *The photocopier machine took years before it was available in the market*

 ## Printer

We all know printers as machines that print documents from a computer. Most printers these days are non-impact devices. This means that they form images using a matrix of tiny dots. The most popular variety of printers is the **laser** printer. It was invented in the 1960s by an engineer named Gary Starkweather (1938–2019).

The laser printer uses a beam of laser light to etch images on a light-conducting drum. The image is then carried from the drum on to paper using electric photocopying. Another popular non-impact printer is the inkjet printer, invented in 1976. This works by spraying electrically charged ink drops directly on to the print paper.

▲ *Some inkjet printers can also print on surfaces other than paper, such as CDs, DVDs, or plastic cards*

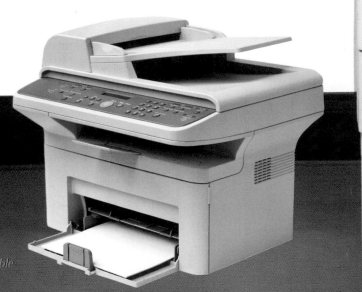

▶ *Most parts in a laser printer cartridge are reusable or recyclable*

★ Incredible Individuals

In the 15th century, a German goldsmith called Johannes Gutenberg (1400–1468) invented the printing press. This was the first machine capable of making multiple copies of pages. The printing press made it faster, easier, and more cost-effective to produce books. This, in turn, allowed all people—not just the rich—to acquire an education. Now that people could read, novels and newspapers became popular.

▲ *Cartridges of a colour printer*

🔍 Fax

The fax machine, also called telefax and facsimile, is a machine that uses wires and radio waves to send and receive messages. These machines scan text or art off paper and transmit the information across phone lines to other machines, where the original document is reproduced on paper.

Over the 19th and 20th centuries, many inventors created and modified this invention. Modern fax machines are cheap, reliable, fast, and easy to use. They almost replaced telegraphic services in offices and homes. They are used as a quick alternative to postal services and couriers.

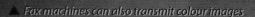

▲ *Fax machines can also transmit colour images*

Computers: A Fruit of the Loom

The idea of a computer first came from weaving. In 1801, French merchant Joseph Jaquard (1752–1834) developed the industrial loom. This machine could weave detailed images on to cloth. Images were stored as punched patterns on cards. Each row of holes was used for a row of threads in the pattern. About 2,000 punch cards were needed for one complete image.

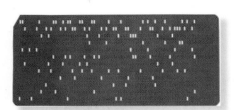

◄ *A used punch card*

🔍 The Personal Computer

Until the 1970s, most people had never come across a computer. At this time, there were two types of computers. One was the large, room-sized version that cost hundreds of thousands of dollars. The other was a mass-produced mini-computer in the similar price range and was used in laboratories and offices. The idea that everyone could have a computer at home—let alone a laptop—was considered a tall tale. What made this possible was the invention of the microprocessor. The processor is what allows the computer to make calculations instantly and respond to your commands. Lots of machines such as cars, dishwashers, TVs, etc., have them today. But the processor of your computer is a great deal more powerful.

🔍 The Future of Computing

In the Internet-linked 21st century, computers are getting smaller and microprocessors more powerful. In a few years, nano-computers could be small enough to fit inside your body to track your health, enhance your abilities, and help you control your surroundings. Experts are already creating environments that are fully computer-controlled. This means your home, car, clothing, and appliances will all respond to your signals. The exciting new field that is powering these possibilities is called quantum computing. This will use the principles of quantum theory—the study of atomic and subatomic particles—to create a new generation of super-fast computers. The full extent of its abilities is yet unimaginable.

◄ *A computer operator with a punch-card sorter at the US Census Bureau (c.1940)*

🔍 The Father of the Computer

British professor Charles Babbage (1791–1871) realised that the punched-card system could also be used to do arithmetic. He modified the loom to create the world's first computer. It was a mechanical invention called the 'Analytical Engine'.

Inventor Herman Hollerith saw Babbage's machine and was inspired to create the 'Hollerith Desk'. The desk used punched cards to gather information from the 1890 American census. Thus, the computer moved beyond calculation to information processing.

▲ *Charles Babbage's brain is on display in the Science Museum in London*

⭐ Incredible Individuals

Ada Lovelace (1815–1852) was a mathematician and the daughter of a famous British poet, Lord Byron. She met Charles Babbage in 1833. Both worked closely to further develop the computer. Among Ada's many contributions was a stepwise sequence for solving certain mathematical problems. For this amazing accomplishment, she is known as the 'world's first computer programmer'.

Ada was also the first to see the vast potential of the Analytical Engine, beyond simple number calculations. She has therefore been called the 'Prophet of the Computer Age'.

◀ *At the age of 12, Lovelace conceptualized a flying machine*

▼ *The 1960s electronic computer URAL-2 was located in Tashkent, Uzbekistan, and relied on vacuum tubes*

The Development of Computers

Computers have come a long way since Babbage and Lovelace first worked on them. Some countries even have super computers to help their governments and scholars with cutting-edge research. The development of computers can be divided into three main periods.

🔍 First Generation Computers: 1937–1946

Dr John Atanasoff and Clifford Berry built the first electronic digital computer in 1937. It was called ABC (Atanasoff-Berry Computer). In 1943, the military had an electronic computer built. They called it the Colossus.

Progress was further made until, in 1946, the first general-purpose computer, the ENIAC was built. Computers of this period did one task at a time and had no operating language or systems.

◀ *The mechanism used to make precise holes on computer punch cards at the US Bureau of the Census (c.1940)*

🔍 Second Generation: 1947–1962

Computers of this period used transistors instead of vacuum tubes. In 1951, UNIVAC 1 (Universal Automatic Computer) became the first computer to be introduced to the public. The first programming languages (about 100 of them) were written for this generation of computers. Storage also became possible through devices such as disks and tapes.

▲ *UNIVAC 1 control station*

🔍 Third Generation: 1963–Present

The invention of the microchip truly revolutionised computers. They became powerful, reliable and a lot smaller. Nowadays, they can run multiple complex programmes at the same time. In 1980, the MS-DOS (Microsoft Disc Operating System) was created.

A year later, IBM introduced the personal computer or PC. Now it was possible to undertake various tasks and even play basic computer games on smaller, more affordable systems. In the 90s, Bill Gates invented the Windows operating system. With this, the PC rapidly became a part of homes and offices across the world.

⭐ Incredible Individuals

The QWERTY keyboard was created by American inventor Christopher Latham Sholes. It was first seen on 1 July 1874.

◀ *A PC from the 1990s*

▲ *The first QWERTY keyboard on a typewriter*

A Timeline of Computer and Mobile Games

1922
Steve Russell, Martin Graetz and Wayne Wiitanen design 'Spacewar!' (Widely considered the first proper computer game)

1952
Alexander Douglas, a student, designs and plays noughts and crosses on Cambridge University's EDSAC computer.

1967
Engineer Ralph Baer tries to use a TV called 'The Brown Box' to play games. It allows users to play games such as table tennis on TV, without a computer. It even had a light gun for shooting games.

1996
High-quality video cards (3dfx chipsets) are launched.

1995
Sony releases the first Play Station console.

1989
Nintendo releases Gameboy which is the first hand-held game console.

1977
Atari launches the first video game console.

1999
EverQuest is created as a Massively Multi-player Online Role-Playing Game (MMORPG).

2006
Nintendo Wii is launched. It introduces new ways of interacting with game systems.

2010
Angry Birds becomes the top-selling mobile phone game.

▲ Controllers used in game consoles

Digital Libraries

A computer and cell phone come with free digital space where one can save documents, movies, music, images, and more. These files can also be saved on external storage devices. Pen drives, DVDs, and hard discs are some examples.

Storage, sometimes called memory is measured in **bytes**. If an external hard disc can store 1 terabyte (TB), that means it can hold about 500 hours' worth of movies. Say a book is 325 pages long; 1 TB would store 264,304 such books. It would take a person several years to get through such a large digital library.

▼ *An audio cassette being inserted into a cassette player*

🔍 Early Storage Devices

▲ *Mark 1 William-Kilburn*

▲ *Atlas magnetic drum*

The first electronic memory device was the 1947 tested Williams-Kilburn tube. Its memory faded in seconds and had to be constantly refreshed. In 1950, the Atlas storage device was invented using a magnetic drum and a rotating cylinder coated in chemicals. This was the first storage type good enough for public use.

New types of storage devices were invented throughout the 50s and the 60s. These included magnetic tapes and disks, metal coils, cartridges, thin films, and photo-digital storage. One notable invention was the floppy disc, also known as the diskette. It was made by IBM in the 1970s and was popular all through the 90s.

▲ *The first floppy disk could store 80kB of data*

🔍 Computer Storage

The various parts of your computer work as a team. Memory is an integral member of this team. It comes into play from the moment you turn on your computer. When you switch it on, the computer loads information from what is called Read-Only Memory (ROM). During this process, the memory controller checks that the computer's memory banks are functioning properly. Next, when you open an application, the computer looks into its Random Access Memory (RAM). The greater your RAM, the faster your computer will work. It is therefore essential not to waste RAM. Your computer will thus load only the most essential feature of an application until more is called for. When you save a file, your computer will find a more permanent memory location for it. Thus, when the application is closed, all files are removed from the RAM.

👤 In Real Life

From 2006 onwards, you could store information online. Companies like Amazon and Dropbox made glossary-based storage available on the Internet. This was called the **Cloud**. A person could simply sign up for it, like a library membership, and store their data online.

Modern Storage: Facts

1984: The floppy disc was replaced by the CD (Compact Disc). The first CD-ROM was released by Sony and Philips. It held the *Grolier's Electronic Encyclopaedia*.

1984: Flash memory was invented by Japanese engineer, Fujio Masuoka. This allowed us to erase old, unwanted data from memory devices and replace it with new data.

1992: Experts needed smaller devices to match the ever-shrinking sizes of computers, phones, and cameras. So, a company called SunDisk (later renamed SanDisk) made the first memory chip.

1995: DVDs (Digital Video Discs) were introduced. For the first time you could store an entire movie in one device.

2000: The USB flash drive, also known as a pen drive or a memory stick, was introduced.

2003: The Blu-ray disc, considered a successor of the DVD, was launched.

2009: The first 1-TB hard disc was invented.

An external storage drive

Pen drives can hold data anywhere between 128 MB to 32 GB (or more)

The Internet of Things

In 1957, the Russians launched the first man-made satellite into space. To push their own technology forward, American President Dwight Eisenhower created the Advanced Research Projects Agency (ARPA) in 1958. Over the next decade, ARPA—with some help from a company called Bolt, Beranek and Neuman (BBN)—created the first computer **network**. This was made of four different computers, running on four different operating systems, and was called ARPANET—the world's first 'Internet'.

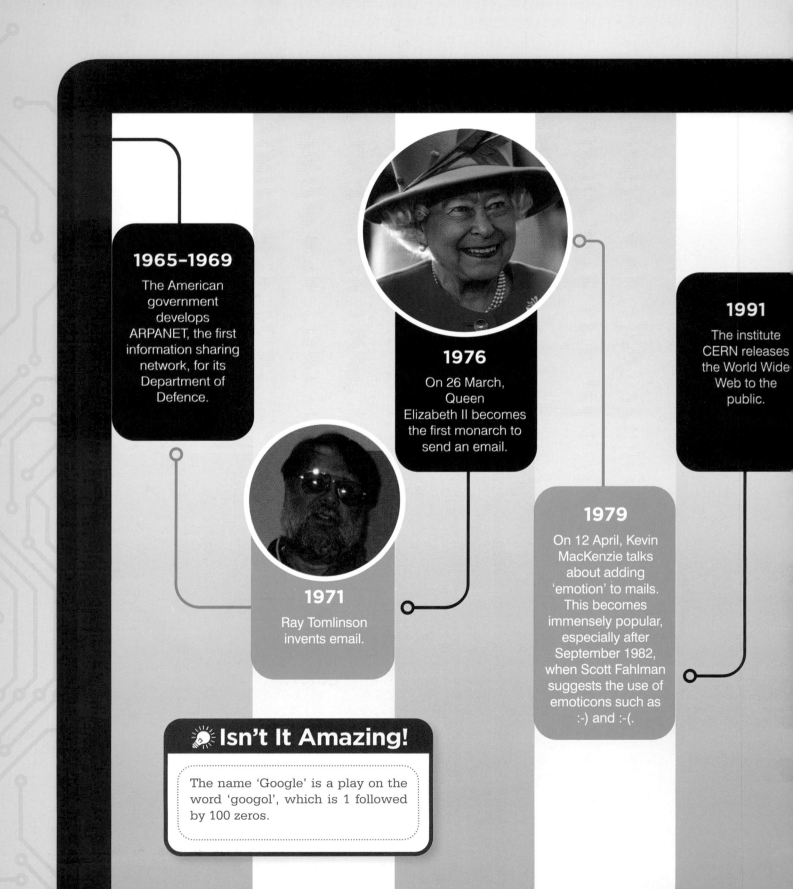

1965–1969
The American government develops ARPANET, the first information sharing network, for its Department of Defence.

1976
On 26 March, Queen Elizabeth II becomes the first monarch to send an email.

1991
The institute CERN releases the World Wide Web to the public.

1971
Ray Tomlinson invents email.

1979
On 12 April, Kevin MacKenzie talks about adding 'emotion' to mails. This becomes immensely popular, especially after September 1982, when Scott Fahlman suggests the use of emoticons such as :-) and :-(.

🔦 Isn't It Amazing!

The name 'Google' is a play on the word 'googol', which is 1 followed by 100 zeros.

The Mother of the Internet

Though she didn't invent the Internet, her many, many contributions to its robust growth make Radia Perlman the 'Mother of the Internet'. Perlman invented a bridge for sharing data that allowed the Internet to handle massive networks. Perlman holds more than 80 patents related to Internet technology, has won many awards—including being named 1 of the 20 most influential people in her field twice, and is part of the Internet Hall of Fame.

▲ *Radia Perlman holds over 100 issued patents*

1995

Amazon, E-bay and Hotmail arrive on the scene. The Vatican goes online. Chris Lamprecht—a 'minor threat' in Texas, USA—becomes the first person to be banned by a court from accessing the Internet.

1996

Larry Page and Sergey Brin develop a search engine called Backrub—later renamed Google!

2004

Facebook goes online and the world of social networking begins.

2016

Google unveils Google Assistant—a 'smart' voice-activated personal assistant software.

1994

The first search engine, Yahoo! is created in April. Shopping malls arrive on the Internet.

Networking

Computer networking allows us to collect, organise, and share all the knowledge in the world with each other. There are two basic types of networks.

LAN

Local-area Networks (LANs) connect machines that are close by. This could be in your house, school, or in an office. The network can be created with wires or fibre-optics. More often, it is done by Ethernet cables or Wi-Fi.

▲ *Network of Ethernet cables at a data centre*

Isn't It Amazing!

In the 1950s, visionary Ted Nelson coined the term 'hyperlink' for the clickable link we see on the web.

WAN

Wide-area Networks (WANs) connect small networks to larger ones, over entire continents. They use cables, optical fibres, and satellites to link up computers. The Internet is the largest WAN.

◀ *Satellite dishes ensure large-scale networking for banks, offices, schools, homes, etc.*

In Real Life

Machines in a LAN follow rules to "talk" to each other. This is called protocol. For instance, if one device signals "I'm ready to send", it must wait until the other responds "I'm ready to receive." With many computers, protocols become complex; this helps avoid network errors.

Ethernet and Wi-Fi

The most popular system for linking computers is the Ethernet. It was created in 1973 by an American team led by Robert Metcalfe. It became available for public use in 1980.

Wireless technology already existed at this time. But Wi-Fi connectivity came in 1997–1999, after tech experts around the world formed the Wireless Ethernet Compatibility Alliance (WECA).

◀ *Wi-Fi uses a router and radio waves to connect computers to a LAN. The signals can only travel short distances—usually less than 100 m*

The World Wide Web and App Stores

The Ethernet became truly useful after the World Wide Web was created. This was done in 1989 by English programmer and physicist Tim Berners-Lee. The web's earliest form had a server, used **HTML** code, and was displayed on the first browser.

In 2009, the mobile phone web came into being. The first one was based on Apple's iTunes. App stores nowadays belong to specific companies. They are run directly on the Internet and are not a part of the World Wide Web.

▶ *Accessing the world through a smartphone has become the modern reality*

The Deep Web

Millions of people around the world use the web for games, news, communication, and more. Yet, people are finding it harder and harder to discover data online. This is because only a tiny portion of the World Wide Web is easily accessible. This is called the Surface Web. It is the part of the web that is accessed by search engines like Google. And it only consists of 0.03 per cent of the information that is truly available! The rest of it is buried in the Deep Web. No one really knows how vast the Deep Web is. Our current technology is simply not strong enough to access all of this material. Some part of the Deep Web, however, is intentionally hidden. This is called the Dark Web.

⊙ Incredible Individuals

In 2009, Chinese-born engineer Charles Kuen Kao (1933–2018) received the Nobel Prize in physics for his discovery in 1966, of how light can be transmitted through fibre-optic cables. Fibre optics use hair-thin, transparent wires. This forms an alternative to Ethernet in creating LANs.

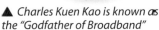

▲ *Charles Kuen Kao is known as the "Godfather of Broadband"*

The Dark Web

Layers and layers of protection are given to information in the Dark Web. It is often used by criminals as well as government spies to hide their activities. It can only be accessed through special codes or browsers. The special software offers privacy and hides the identity of the user. Thus, it offers security for people who deal with information and goods and services, whether legal or illegal. On the bright side, the Dark Web allows greater freedom to people who live in dictatorial and totalitarian nations. It is also routinely used to leak information about political and organisational wrongdoings, so that powerful but corrupt people are brought to justice.

Artificial Intelligence

Alan Mathison Turing (1912–1954) was a British computer scientist who contributed immensely to our knowledge of mathematics, secret codes, logic, and philosophy. During World War II, Turing described a machine that could scan its own memory and modify its behaviour. Essentially, it would 'reason' from the information it was given.

▲ *Alan Mathison Turing is the Father of Modern Computer Science*

1939

Elektro is the first human-like robot ever seen. He can move his arms and legs, and 'knows' a few jokes.

1961

UNIMATE becomes the first mass-produced industrial robot. It looks like a giant arm and weighs over 1,800 kg.

1976

Inspired by elephant trunks, the Soft Gripper robot gently adjusts its shape to the object it is holding.

1956

Computer scientist John McCarthy coins the term '**Artificial Intelligence**'.

1965

DENDRAL is the first AI programme to use a series of 'if-then' rules to make correct decisions.

1941

Author Isaac Asimov describes the Three Laws of Robotics. This is the first known use of the word 'robotics'.

1950–1951

Small, wheeled robots like Elsie and Squee are programmed to show 'behaviour'.

The Turing Test

In 1951, Turing created a test for such machines. He proposed that if you cannot tell the difference between answers given by humans and answers given by the machine, then the machine must be thinking. Turing therefore changed the way human beings think about intelligence. Today Artificial Intelligence or AI can not only learn, reason, and solve problems, it can also interact with its surroundings, as we do, and behave accordingly.

1989
AI programme Deep Thought defeats chess master David Levy.

2004
NASA sends two robots— Spirit and Opportunity— to Mars.

2002
Roomba becomes the first robotic vacuum cleaner.

1995
Robotics is now used in military aircrafts. The MQ-1 Predator drone is an unmanned American plane spying over Afghanistan and Pakistan.

2005
AI is used to make self-driving cars.

1984
The first robot toy, Hero Jr, can play games, sing songs, and be your alarm clock. It roams beside you as it 'likes' to stay near humans.

2000
ASIMO walks, runs, and climbs steps like humans. It reacts correctly to human faces and gestures.

1966
ELIZA can trick people into thinking she is a real doctor!

1999
AIBO—a robotic dog—'learns' and responds to over 100 voice commands. Sometimes, it even ignores you like your real pet!

2011
Siri becomes the first of many AI programmes to be introduced to mobile phones.

INVENTIONS IN MOTION

INVENTIONS THAT MOVED US

Until the Industrial Age, which began more than 250 years ago, people were dependent on animal-drawn machines for labour and travel. Oxen and mules were put to work in farms and mills, while horses pulled carriages across town and country. Travel to distant lands was largely the privilege of aristocrats, merchants, and soldiers who could either afford to travel or had their travel expenses paid for by their employers.

All of this changed when human beings invented **locomotive** engines. These mechanical marvels led to a plethora of machines that could power themselves. From the basic steam engine to the powerful jet and modern electric engines, these inventions in motion are at the heart of modern ease and exploration.

A Balancing Act

The first transport invention that may be called a bicycle had two wheels but no pedals. It was the wooden **draisienne**, invented by a German named Baron Karl von Drais de Sauerbrun (1785–1851). In 1817, he pushed and rode it for 14 kms, proving that it was possible to balance on two wheels while moving forward.

In 1818, some 300 modified draisiennes, called hobby-horses and **velocipedes**, were brought out by another inventor based in London called Denis Johnson. People found them expensive and difficult to use. Riders were even laughed at on the streets! Naturally, they went out of style quickly, but the idea of the cycle remained of interest to inventors. For the next 40 years, inventors created different kinds of three-wheeled and four-wheeled cycles.

◀ The draisienne was made of wood and had no pedals. The riders moved by propelling themselves forward against the ground, much like Fred Flintstone in his 'car'

▲ Three-wheeled velocipedes, developed during the 1880s, were more stable than the draisienne and some could carry multiple passengers

▼ A **Victorian** couple on a **quadricycle** (four-wheeled cycle) designed for two people

⊙ Incredible Individuals

Early safety bicycles had solid rubber tyres. Though better than plain wooden tyres, these were still not very good shock absorbers. At the time, a Scottish vet by the name John Boyd Dunlop (1840–1921) was looking to make his son's tricycle less bumpy to ride. In 1887, he got the brilliant idea of pumping air into hollow rubber tubes. He is, thus, the inventor of the **pneumatic** tyre, which is used in all bicycles today.

▲ John Boyd Dunlop speeding along on pneumatic tyres

Pedalling to Fame

The first cycle with pedals was completed by a blacksmith named Kirkpatrick Macmillan (1812–1878) in Scotland in the 1840s. He felt that the cycle would be more usable if people could propel it forward without placing their feet on the ground.

By 1868, Europe had named velocipedes with pedals as bicycles. They were now being built out of cast iron instead of wood. Bicycles were made popular by the Olivier brothers, Rene and Aime, of France. In 1865, they pedalled a record 800 km from Paris to Marseille. Their enthusiasm caught on and cycling became a popular sport among the young and the rich.

In Real Life

The penny-farthing was a boneshaker with an oversized front wheel that was better at handling bad roads. One of its riders was the world champion cyclist William 'Plugger' Martin (1860–1942), who won a six-day race in New York in 1891.

▲ Early bicycles like the Oliviers' had wood-spoked wheels and iron rims. They were so jarring to ride, people called them boneshakers

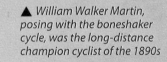

▲ William Walker Martin, posing with the boneshaker cycle, was the long-distance champion cyclist of the 1890s

◄ The 1885 Rover Safety was designed by John Kemp Starley. It was the first bicycle to offer true advantages in stability, braking, and easy mounting

Ingenious Engines

Although we use electrical energy to power gadgets, we rarely use it to physically move objects. The prime movers in our world are engines. Most engines use either steam power or a process called internal combustion. Both types of engines are powerful technologies that came up during the 18th and 19th centuries.

▲ Invented by Hero of Alexandria in the first century CE, the aeolipile is the first known steam-driven mechanism. It is named after Aeolus, the Greek god of air

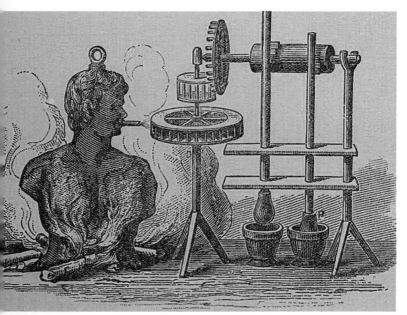

◀ Giovanni Branca's designs showed how the weight of air in the form of steam could be used to move gears and pistons, and thus do mechanical work. However, the method used by this machine was deemed wasteful

A Slow Start

Steam engines have been around since Hero of Alexandria built one called the aeolipile, about 2,000 years ago. Unfortunately, his invention was more or less ignored as a trivial toy. Then, Taqi al-Din—in 1551, and Giovanni Branca—in 1629, described rudimentary **turbines** driven by steam power. These did not actually work on anything; they were just meant to show people how powerful steam could be.

▼ In 1802, 'Charlotte Dundas' became the first successful steamboat. It was built by William Symington

Raising Steam

The first steam engine of practical use was patented by a British inventor named Thomas Savery (1650-1715) in 1698. The purpose was to 'raise water by fire'. It was used to raise water from underground mines. The machine worked by heating water until it turned into vapour. This vapour or steam moved to a higher container. As the steam condensed, it created a vacuum that drew up the water—similar to how you suck water through a straw. But there was little else that this steam engine could do. Also, it was a dangerous machine. The cylinder could burst in cases of excess steam! Imagine your pressure cooker blowing your kitchen to smithereens. Now imagine the havoc caused by an industrial-sized pressure chamber.

▲ A part of Savery's steam pump

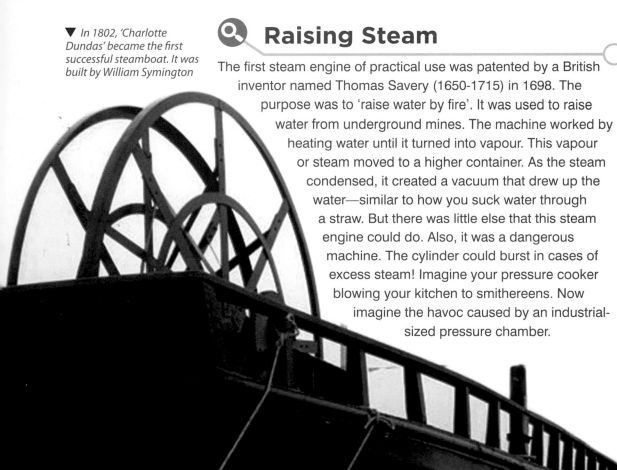

🔍 The Industrial Age Wonder

In 1712, Thomas Newcomen (1664–1729) developed a better steam engine. James Watt (1736–1819) further improved it in 1765. Most importantly, Watt added a rotating shaft that produced wheel-like circular movements instead of simple up-down, pump-like movements. At this point, the steam engine became immensely useful. Inventors used it to build the first locomotives—vehicles that were not pulled by animals— and kicked off the revolutionary Industrial Age!

◄ In 1802, Richard Trevithick (1771–1833) built the first steam locomotive. It ran on a horse-drawn tram route

► Robert Fulton (1765–1815) built the first commercially successful steamboat

⭐ Incredible Individuals

George Stephenson (1781–1848), the self-educated son of a coal-mine mechanic, pioneered the railway locomotive. His steam engine was so revolutionary, the people of Stockton locked their homes and came down to see it. The Prime Minister himself travelled in it. Though famous, Stephenson was a quiet man who refused most honours offered to him, including a knighthood and a seat in the Parliament.

▲ Stephenson's Rocket won the Rainhill Trials of the Liverpool and Manchester Railway in 1829

▼ In 1829, engineer George Stephenson invented the railway engine. The Rocket, as it was called, became a worldwide success

What is Internal Combustion?

Combustion is simply another word for burning. Since the burning happens inside the engine, it is called internal combustion. An internal combustion engine can burn fuels such as gas, petrol, or diesel to move large objects like cars and planes. There are many types of Internal Combustion Engines (ICEs), to match the many types of vehicles we use.

The Four-stroke Engine

The first successful Internal Combustion Engine was built by Belgian inventor Etienne Lenoir (1822–1900) around 1860. It looked like a horizontal steam engine, but used an explosive mix of gases set afire by an electric spark.

The heat and pressure from the burning fuel pushed pistons and wheels, and got the machine moving. Lenoir's engine was expensive until 1878, when German inventor Nikolaus Otto (1832–1891) added refinements that made it more reasonably available.

| 1. Intake | 2. Compression | 3. Fuel power | 4. Fuel Exhaust |

▲ *Otto's ICE worked in four steps (or strokes)—intake of air and fuel, compression of the mix, firing of the mix, and release of the exhaust*

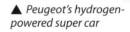
▲ *Peugeot's hydrogen-powered super car*

Isn't It Amazing!

Back in 1780, Alessandro Volta (1745–1827), who invented the battery, built a pistol. He did not develop it as a weapon, but rather as an experiment. In fact, it was pretty useless as a weapon.

Volta's Pistol, as it was called, used an electric spark to ignite a mix of air and fuel—hydrogen, thus using the same principle as today's car engines. Of course, pistols became much more advanced after that.

▶ *An illustration of Alessandro Volta discussing electricity with Napoleon Bonaparte*

The Diesel Engine

Rudolf Diesel (1858–1913) of Germany came across Otto's engine soon after it was invented. He set about making it more efficient and developed his 'combustion-powered engine'. In 1892, the government recognised it as the diesel engine.

Although this was truly a powerful engine, it was noisy, smelly—due to noxious exhaust fumes, and worked best at lower speeds. Over the 20th century, most countries banned diesel engines from small vehicles. Today, we see them largely in heavy goods carriers such as trucks, ships, and road trains.

Smaller and Faster

In 1885, Germans Gottlieb Daimler (1834–1900) and Wilhelm Maybach (1846–1929) famously invented an engine that resembled a "grandfather clock", hence it was called the grandfather clock engine. It was the first small, high-speed ICE to run on petrol. It was the grandfather of all modern petrol engines. Daimler and Maybach fitted it on to a number of vehicles, including a cycle, a stagecoach, and a boat.

▲ *Daimler and Maybach's "grandfather clock engine"*

Engines and Pollution

Our engines release toxic gases into the air, such as carbon dioxide—the main cause of catastrophic climate change—or sulphur dioxide and nitrogen oxides, which cause acid rain, breathing problems, and ozone depletion, among other issues. Hence, it is important to use engines that are good for the environment. These engines should use less harmful fuels like hydrogen, liquefied petroleum gas (LPG), and biodiesel. Electric cars with solar-powered cells or batteries may be the 'cleanest' engine on the horizon.

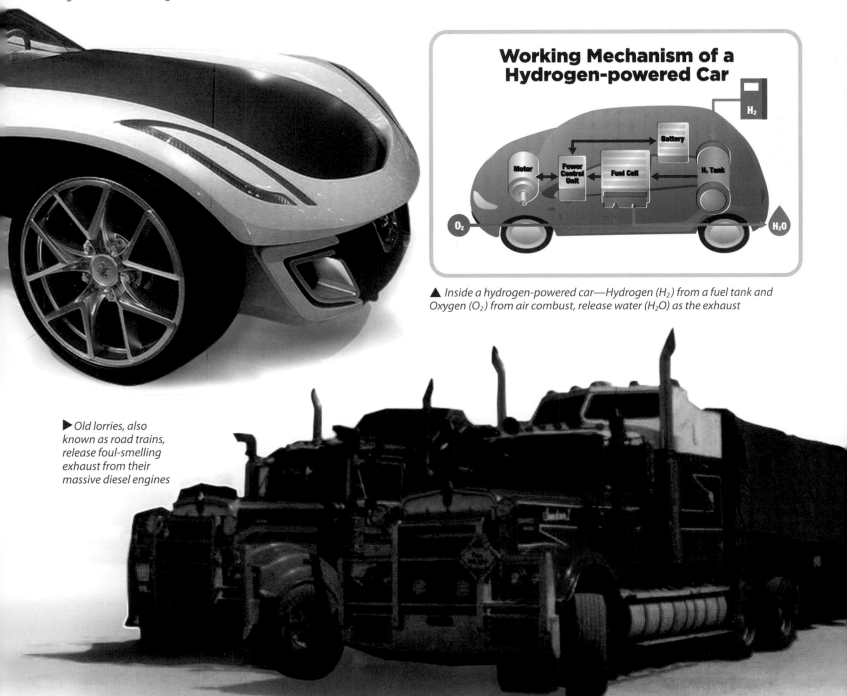

Working Mechanism of a Hydrogen-powered Car

Motor — Power Control Unit — Fuel Cell — Battery — H₂ Tank — O₂ — H₂O

▲ *Inside a hydrogen-powered car—Hydrogen (H_2) from a fuel tank and Oxygen (O_2) from air combust, release water (H_2O) as the exhaust*

▶*Old lorries, also known as road trains, release foul-smelling exhaust from their massive diesel engines*

The First Cars

In the early 20th century, nearly 80 per cent of all American cars ran on either steam or electricity. Petrol cars were noisy, shaky, and often broke down. Steam cars too had many complications. In contrast, electric cars were easy to start, silent, and needed little maintenance. Unfortunately, the ever-polluting petrol car squashed out its competition over time. It has dominated our roads ever since.

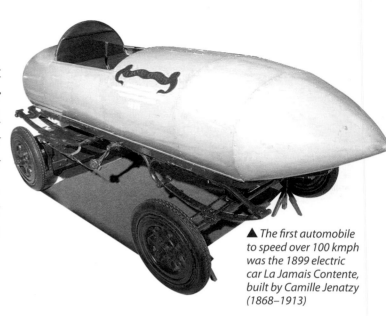

▲ The first automobile to speed over 100 kmph was the 1899 electric car La Jamais Contente, built by Camille Jenatzy (1868–1913)

▲ In the Motorwagen, the passengers and the engine sat above two wheels; the front wheel steered the car

▼ Benz invented the Victoria with four wheels. He wanted the car to be priced low enough for mass production, so more people could buy automobiles

🔍 Karl Benz and the Petrol Car

The car is a complex creature. Its many parts are the brainchildren of different people. However, Karl Friedrich Benz (1844–1929) of Germany is considered the inventor of the first 'true' automobile which was powered by gasoline. Called the Motorwagen, this three-wheeled car was built in 1885.

Benz also invented the **accelerator**, the battery-operated ignition, the **spark plug**, the **gear shift**, the **water radiator**, the **clutch**, the **carburettor**, and the axle-pivot steering system. In 1896, he designed a high-performance engine that is still used in racing cars today!

💡 Isn't It Amazing!

Early cars were quite different from the ones we see today. The Motorwagen of early 1888 was pushed, not driven, up sloping roads and hills. Early car owners had to buy petrol at pharmacies where it was sold as a cleaning product. Naturally, they did not have it in large supply. Interestingly, the first Benz car was bought in the summer of 1888.

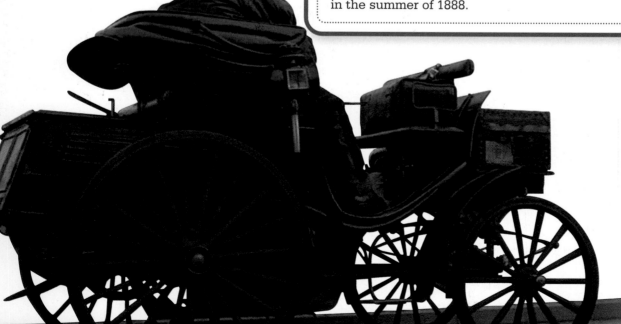

◀ *The photograph shows a reconstruction of da Vinci's self-propelled cart. Renaissance genius Leonardo da Vinci designed and described an automobile way back in 1509*

In Real Life

Some countries historically banned women from driving. Locomotion has given humankind a great deal of freedom of movement, and some people wanted to withhold this freedom from women. In June 2018, Saudi Arabia became the last remaining country to lift the ban on female drivers.

◀ *A poster from Saudi Arabia's #women2drive movement*

Incredible Individuals

The story goes that Benz's wife, Bertha, once secretly took the Motorwagen to visit her mother, who lived 106 km away. Bertha started the drive on the morning of 5 August, 1888 and brought along her sons Eugene and Richard.

On the way, she had to hunt for fuel at pharmacies and overcome numerous technical and mechanical problems. The trio finally arrived at night and sent off a telegram to Benz announcing their achievement! The event is now celebrated every year in Germany with an antique automobile rally.

Bertha Benz
Memorial Rcute

▶ *One of the official signposts along the 194 km long Bertha Benz Memorial Route, in memory of 'man's' first long-distance car journey*

▲ *Henry Ford (1863–1947) launched his famous Model T in 1908. This low-priced, easy-to-maintain car revolutionised the industry by turning cars into daily necessities; earlier, they were seen as luxury items*

▼ *France's motor industry began in 1890 with cars made by Armand Peugeot (1849–1915) and Emile Levassor (1843–1897). Peugeot cars were seen at this 1901 Paris Motor Show*

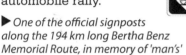

Collectable Cars

Sometime over the years 1925–1928, fast luxury motorcars became status symbols. Considered to be classic cars, these are now highly valued by collectors. However, every decade since then has seen technical and mechanical advances, producing cars of greater efficiency, and sheer beauty.

◄ This 1929 Phantom belongs to Rolls Royce, whose brand is synonymous with limousines and luxury sedans

▶ Aston Martin, the British luxury automobile, is the most famous for being James Bond's car

Racing Cars

Car racing is one of the world's most extreme and exciting sport. Organised racing began in 1894 with an 80 km race. The spirit of competition soon led to special cars being invented just for racing. The technological advancement that came forth in racing hugely benefitted the manufacture of civilian cars. It also advanced our discoveries in **aerodynamics**. In the years following WWII, Europe saw the rise of Formula One (F1) racing. Nowadays, F1 cars are some of the fastest racing cars in the world.

▼ By the 1950s, Jaguar was building sleek and powerful sportscars like the C-type racer

▶ The Bugatti Type 35, one of the early cars was built specifically for racing

▼ Reaching a speed of 301 kmph, the Hennessy Venom GT is the fastest series-produced road car

Breaking Speed Records

On 8 March 1886, Daimler and Maybach secretly brought home a stagecoach, telling their neighbours it was a birthday gift for Mrs Daimler. With the help of their grandfather clock engine, they turned it into the first four-wheeled automobile to reach a speed of 16 kmph. Today, the fastest vehicle on land is the Thrust SSC. On 15 October 1997, American Andy Green drove it at speeds faster than sound, making it a supersonic car!

▶ Set up in Italy in the 1960s, Lamborghini is known today for its top-of-the-line sports cars. Like all Lamborghinis, this 2011 Aventador is named after a fighting bull

▶ The Thrust SSC reached speeds of 1227.985 kmph in the Black Rock Desert of Nevada, USA

A World on Track

A train is a long string of cars, or carriages that is pulled along by an engine. It transports either people or goods from place to place. There are many different kinds of trains, such as monorails, funiculars, turbo trains, bullet trains, double-deckers, and even 'toy' trains.

▶ The toy train of Darjeeling (India) runs on narrow rails along the Himalayas. This railway is now a UNESCO World Heritage Site

▲ A double-decker hi-speed train in France

Passenger Trains

Trains that carry people over long distances are called passenger trains. They are powered by diesel engines. Faster, modern passenger trains are powered by electricity. Long-distance trains are designed to be comfortable. Their seats often double up as beds. They also have plenty of luggage space. Some passenger trains even have dining cars.

City Trains

A commuter or city train carries large numbers of people over short distances. They are most often used to travel between work and home. Commuter trains have a lot of standing space, which allows them to carry more people during each trip. Seating and luggage space are minimal. Most commuter trains run on electricity.

▲ The commuter trains of Mumbai, India, carry hundreds of thousands of passengers each day

Metros

Another way of travelling in large cities is the metro system. This consists of electrically powered trains that run on tracks which are either underground or flyovers. Metro trains can accelerate much faster than long-distance trains.

▲ London metro tube

Monorails

The monorail is a special type of metro. It consists of a single track instead of two parallel rail tracks. The train straddles the track, that is, covers it from side to side. Sometimes, the track runs above the train! In such cases, the train is suspended from the track.

▲ Tokyo Monorail

Freight Trains

Freight trains are also called goods trains. These are used to transport overland cargo. Traditionally, workers would load the cargo into box wagons. Nowadays, cranes lift large containers of goods into and out of the wagons. Sometimes, trucks carrying goods drive on to the freight trains. At their destination, the trucks disembark and continue onwards by road.

▼ A freight train carrying cargo containers

To Keep the Wheels Turning

Another exciting form of transport is the motorcycle. It provides the flexibility of a bicycle along with the convenience of a car! In November 1885, Daimler installed a smaller version of the grandfather clock engine on a wooden bicycle, creating the first two-wheeled petrol-powered motorcycle. It was named the Reitwagen (the riding car). Daimler's partner Maybach rode it for 3 km by the River Neckar, reaching speeds of 12 kmph.

◀ *In 1884, Edward Butler built the first commercial motorcycle. It had three wheels and ran on petrol*

🔍 Evolving Motorcycles

In the early 1900s, inventors everywhere were attaching engines to cycles and creating their own versions of the motorcycle. A lot of them were sold on the streets and were called touring machines.

In an effort to discover top-notch bikes, the first motorcycle races were set up at the Isle of Man. Of these, the 1907-established Tourist Trophy (TT) race became the most famous and most extreme form of bike racing in the world.

▲ *The BAT twin-cylinder motorcycle of 1910 set a new track record of 80 kmph at the TT race*

🔍 Springing to Action

Nowadays, motorcycles come in a variety of designs depending on what you need them for. People enjoy riding motorcycles for long journeys, navigating city roads, adventure biking, and racing, to name just a few.

▲ *By the end of WWI, Harley Davidson was the largest motorcycle manufacturer, selling in 67 countries*

⭐ Incredible Individuals

Born on 17 November 1906, Soichiro Honda (1906–1991) was the pioneering force behind Honda motorcycles, one of the largest motorcycle manufacturers today. Starting out as a teenage mechanic, he began inventing automobile parts during WWII. Over his lifetime, he gained recognition for over 100 inventions!

In 1945, he founded what eventually became the Honda Motor Company, which built light motorcycles that ran on small but efficient engines. By the 1980s, Honda was the third-largest Japanese automaker.

Honda himself had strong ethics. He built close relationships with his workers. He stood firm against the government when it tried to limit Japan's auto industry. And even in his 60s, he was still personally testing new models of motorcycles.

▲ *Soichiro Honda had no formal education*

▼ *Nowadays, the Japanese manufacturers Honda, Yamaha, Kawasaki, and Suzuki dominate the world of motorcycles*

The Omnibus Edition

The modern word 'bus' is short for the older word, 'omnibus', where the Latin 'omnis' means 'for all'. Hence, these large cars were meant for all people. Omnibuses were originally drawn by horses.

The Popular Omnibus

When locomotives took off, not everyone could buy an expensive motorcar. The first motorised road-transport for the public came in the form of trams. In 1834, Thomas Davenport (1802–1851), an American blacksmith, found a way to drive a battery-powered car on tracks. In the 1860s, this idea was expanded into tramways that carried electrical passenger-cars on tracks.

▲ Horse-drawn buses, called omnibuses, have been around a long time. They can still be seen in England

From Tram to Bus

The problem with trams is that, like trains, their routes are rigidly fixed. Also, they are suitable only for smooth town or city roads. People had to use stagecoaches to travel through the countryside at the time.

In 1830, Sir Goldworthy Gurney (1793–1875) powered a large stagecoach using a steam engine. This was likely the world's first motorbus. Petrol engines were used in buses about 60 years later, starting in Germany. Over 1905–1962 buses in Berlin actually pulled trailers to carry more passengers. Today, buses are the only feasible mode of transportation for many families who cannot afford cars or are environment-conscious.

▲ Trams are powered by electrified wires that ran overhead along the length of the tramlines

Modern Buses

Numerous types of buses have been invented over the years, but we recognise four main categories: the city bus, the double-decker bus, the long-distance tour bus, and the school bus. The double-decker is the much-beloved giant among buses and is occasionally seen in cities. Open-roofed double-deckers are often run by tourist companies to ferry people around landmark sights in cities like London. School buses are mostly run by private companies. They follow the system of public transportation, while halting at a certain point where the parents come to collect their children. Long-distance buses might be private or government-run.

▶ City buses often have low maximum speeds, two entrances, and no luggage space

◀ A double-decker bus

To Reap What We Sow

Farming is one of the hardest, noblest jobs on the planet; it supports billions of lives. Inventions in agriculture are therefore of great importance to humankind. Since the start of the Industrial Age, some 200 odd years ago, various machines have been created to reduce the burden of work on farmers. Key among them are machines that can harvest, thresh, and winnow or clean grain-producing crops.

▲ *Combine harvesters were first seen in the 1830s. For nearly 100 years, they needed horse power to operate*

🔍 The Combine Harvester

A working vehicle that combines four separate harvesting operations—reaping, threshing, gathering, and winnowing—is called a combine harvester. The earliest combine harvesters were pulled along by large teams of horses or mules—sometimes as many as 30 horses! Nowadays, harvesters run on internal combustion engines like most vehicles on the road.

🔍 To Sow, so We May Reap

The tractor is a farm vehicle with enormous rear wheels. It is used to pull heavy machinery for ploughing, planting, tilling, and various such activities. Traction engines used to be powerful steam-powered machines that drew heavy loads and ploughs over rough ground. They were a modification of portable steam engines used on farms in the late 19th century. The first farm vehicle to run on a petrol-powered engine was invented in 1892 by John Froehlich (1849–1933), an American blacksmith. By WWI, tractors had become a common sight. In fact, the US Holt model even inspired the creation of WWI military tanks.

▲ *Featured here is a steam-powered tractor. Early tractors had steel tyres with numerous projections. This helped the vehicle grip the ground and pull its load forward. Tractors with oversized rubber tyres first appeared in 1932 and rapidly became a standard feature*

▼ *A modern combine harvester uses different types of detachable 'heads' to meet its functions. This harvester is using a wide-mouthed reaper to harvest a field*

🔍 Optimum Agriculture

Farming has become so advanced, it even uses space technology! Specifically, farmers can now buy tractors with GPS and sophisticated computers. This allows tractors to function like drones.

For instance, using information from satellites, the vehicle is able to plough land in a precise way. There is no overlap, no missed land, and no wastage of fuel.

Army on Wheels

The first armoured locomotive was built in 1900 in England. It ran on steam engines and hauled supplies during the Second Boer War (1899–1902) of South Africa. The first motorised weapon-carrier had been built a year earlier. This was a quadricycle mounted with a machine gun. It was not long before inventors began putting armour and motor together to create formidable vehicles for military forces across the globe.

▶ British inventor Fredrick Simms (1863–1944) on his gun-toting 'motor scout'

Barrelling Through Enemy Lines

Tanks were first seen during WWI. They were deployed by the British against the Germans in September 1916. Between the two armies lay the fearsome 'no man's land' of Somme—a hellish marsh of bombed trenches, barbed wire, and dying soldiers. Neither army was able to move forward. That is, until the British Mark I tanks arrived on the scene. Equipped with machine guns and running on chain-like tracks, they were able to cross the trenches and wires, and effectively support their soldiers. The clear advantage offered that day fuelled the beginning of tank warfare!

▲ A Mark I tank in the Chimpanzee Valley on 15 September 1916, the first day of battle for the tanks

The Amphibious Assault Vehicle (AAV)

In 1935, engineer Donald Roebling (1908–1959) built a lightweight aluminium vehicle that worked both in water and on land. Named the Alligator, it was used as a rescue vehicle. At the time, the US Marine Corps was looking for a tank-like vehicle to protect its soldiers during beach landings. Inspired by the Alligator, they built a powerful steel-plated version in 1941. This was the LVT (Landing Vehicle Tracked). So useful was the invention, that some 18,620 LVTs were made during WWII. Continuous improvements took place over the next few decades and other countries built their own designs. By 1985, the US had renamed it the Amphibious Assault Vehicle.

▼ An AAV of the Assault Amphibian Battalion, 2nd Marine Division, making its way into the water, in 2011

Smart Mobility

Modern vehicles have made the world a closely connected place. However, they have also created some troubling issues. Think traffic jams, noise pollution, global warming, oil spills in the ocean, mining hazards, and health concerns from air pollution.

▲ *The Tesla Roadster, an electric sports car*

🔍 Electric Cars

Electric cars were invented in the 19th century. They can be energy efficient; they do not create air or noise pollution; and they do not need expensive fuels like petrol. Despite this, the first mass-produced car to run on electricity was launched only in 1997. This was Japan's Toyota Prius. Since then, many automobile companies have joined the race to invent better electric cars and set up charging points, so people can 'refuel' conveniently. In addition, batteries are becoming more powerful, so cars can travel farther on a single charge, and also recharge at a faster pace.

▲ *Socket for an electric car battery charger*

▶ *An electric car charging point in Germany*

🔍 Self-driving Vehicles

Our cars are already chock-full of advanced technology for easy travel. For instance, modern cars feature satellites and GPS to help find the destination and guide the driver there on the shortest route with the least traffic. But this is just the beginning of smart vehicles.

Many automobile and technology companies are inventing cars that can function without a human driver. These self-driving or automated cars use a mix of radar, laser, GPS, and other sensors and technologies to safely navigate roads. Of course, this is not limited to cars. Delivery trucks may also soon be fully automated. In early 2018, Starsky Robotics's self-driving truck became the first of its kind to safely make an 11-km journey on a public road, without a driver.

▲ *We may soon have cars that can sense pedestrians and other vehicles and maintain a safe distance from them. This would greatly increase road safety*

▶ *Google's self-driving car*

Maglev Trains

Maglev is short for magnetic levitation. The name is used for high-speed trains that move while floating over **electromagnetic** tracks. Maglevs do not have an engine. Instead, they have powerful magnets below the train. When electricity passes through the railway track or guideway, it becomes magnetised, and repels the magnets below the train. The reaction is so strong that the entire train is lifted just above the guideway.

If you have seen magnets, you know that like poles repel and opposite poles attract. This rule is used to create a system of power at the front of the train, causing it to move forward to its destination.

 # Making Maglevs

Maglev trains were first thought of by Robert Goddard (1882–1945) and French-born engineer Emile Bachelet (1863–1946). The first Maglev train for public use was built in 1984–1985, in the United Kingdom, between Birmingham airport and a nearby station.

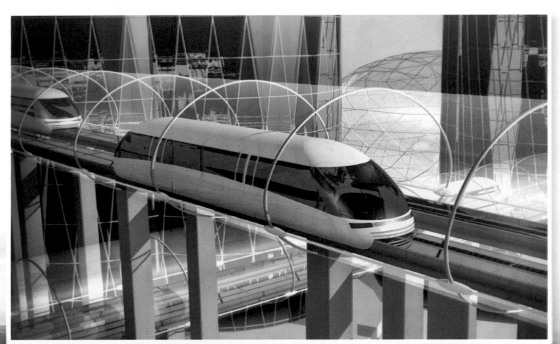

◀ The Hyperloop—a special kind of Maglev, currently under construction—travels at speeds up to 1,080 kmph inside a fully enclosed, near-vacuum tube

▼ The longest Maglev today is in Shanghai. It is 30 km long and transports people from downtown Shanghai to Pudong International Airport. The system that uses magnets to repel the train from the track is called an electrodynamic suspension (EDS) system

Ships Ahoy!

Human beings have been using rowing boats since prehistoric times. The first sailboats were seen on the River Nile and belonged to the ancient Egyptians. By the Iron Age, ships were large enough to carry several tonnes of cargo between prosperous trading port cities.

Until the Industrial Age, all river and seafaring vessels, large and small, were powered either by oars or by wind sails. The speed of a sea craft is measured in knots. A speed of 1 knot means the boat is travelling at 1.8 kmph.

In Real Life

Did you know, Queen Elizabeth I of England had an official person who uncorked 'ocean bottles'? His duty was to open messages from bottles that washed ashore. This was a serious and important job! In fact, it was a capital crime for anyone else to do this, as the Queen believed that these seafaring secrets may have come from spies abroad.

The trireme was the deadliest warship of the 5th century BCE. It needed 170 oarsmen arranged in three rows, one above the other, to propel the ship.

In the 16th century, the Chinese were inspired by Portuguese treasure ships to build their own galleys, called Wugongchuan (centipede ships).

All at Sea

After 1200, sailing ships truly came into their own. The stern rudder was invented to guide the ship more firmly. Deep-draft hulls were successfully engineered to hold more cargo and speed across oceans.

By the 14th century, shipbuilding got so specialised that warships became separate from merchant vessels. From the 15th century onwards, ships also had multiple masts and complex arrangements of sails.

Christopher Columbus's 15th century ship, named *Santa Maria*, was the flagship on his first voyage to the Americas.

Queen Anne's Revenge was the ship of the most famous pirate, Blackbeard.

▼ *Viking longships terrorised the European seas for more than 1,500 years. During the Dark Ages, these boats carried warriors from the icy north to plunder and colonise new lands*

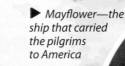

▶ *Mayflower—the ship that carried the pilgrims to America*

🔍 Making Waves

Steam-propelled boats were first seen during the late 1700s. Some of them worked and some did not. By the early 19th century, American inventor Robert Fulton (1765–1815) had developed steamboats that were strong enough for commercial use. He also built the US Navy's first steam warship, the *Demologos*. These vessels moved using steam-powered paddles arranged in the form of a wheel, at the boat's side or stern. The paddle was later replaced by the screw propeller, which was more resistant to storm damage and easier to steer with. Eventually, screw propellers were combined with steam-turbine engines, as seen in modern steamships. By WWI, coal and oil were also being used as fuel.

The famous *Titanic* was powered by multistage steam turbines, an 1894 invention of Sir Charles Algernon Parsons (1854–1931), who first used them in the yacht *Turbina*.

The 19th century paddle steamer, *Queen Victoria*.

The 1843 built *SS Great Britain* was the first ship to have a full iron hull. Iron-clad warships were extensively used in the American Civil War (1861–1865).

🔍 Military Matters

During WWII—and even after it—a great number of ships were constructed with ever-advancing technology. Such vessels served naval forces both as warships and cargo vessels. Many technologies made their way into luxury cruisers and merchant ships. While steam engines continued to run passenger ships, diesel and oil engines became popular for freighters. Earlier inventions such as radars also went through refinements.

▲ In 1910, the USS Birmingham became the first ship to launch an aeroplane. Eight years later, HMS Argus became the first true aircraft carrier that could transport, launch, and land aeroplanes

🔍 Radar

Radar is a type of active electromagnetic sensor. It is used for finding, identifying, and tracking objects that are far away. The objects are usually air or sea crafts and weapons. The radar works by sending out electromagnetic waves through the air and listening for any echoes that come back. The waves sent out are usually microwaves, which are very similar to what heats your food at home.

Oil tankers are the behemoths of the ocean. This supertanker can carry 2 million barrels of crude oil.

Under the Sea

Submarines are closed ships that move both on and under water. They were first used as weapons during the American War of Independence (1775–1783). But it was only in WWI, when Germany used them to fire torpedoes at merchant ships, that submarines acquired a fearsome image. The modern nuclear-powered submarines first appeared in the 1960s. They are able to stay underwater for several months at a time and are armed with some of the deadliest weapons known to humankind.

🔍 Early Submarines

British mathematician William Bourne (c. 1535-1582) was the first to seriously think about an underwater ship or a submarine. In 1578, he wrote of an enclosed, waterproof boat that could dive beneath water and row through it.

The first person to build such a machine was Dutch inventor Cornelius van Drebel (1572–1633). Over 1620–1624, he tried out his vessel in the River Thames. So successful were his trials, even King James I of England went into his submarine for a short ride!

◀ In 1800–1801, steamboat inventor Robert Fulton built a submarine called *Nautilus* for Napoleon Bonaparte. Made from copper and iron, it held enough air to support four men and two burning candles for three hours

🔍 In Deep Waters

In the late 1800s, submarines became more powerful with the help of steam turbine engines and internal combustion engines. The first submarine ever to run on a battery-powered motor was called *Nautilus* (not to be confused with Fulton's machine). Germany's infamous U-boats—from the German word *Unterseeboot*—were the terror of WWI. The U-1 was built in 1905. It revolutionised the way submarines worked. The machine used a diesel engine to move on water, but a battery to move under water. This became the standard for submarines until the end of WWII.

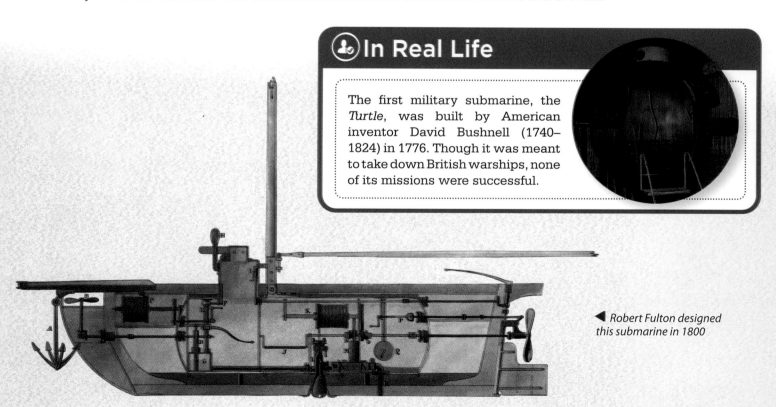

👤 In Real Life

The first military submarine, the *Turtle*, was built by American inventor David Bushnell (1740–1824) in 1776. Though it was meant to take down British warships, none of its missions were successful.

◀ Robert Fulton designed this submarine in 1800

Nuclear Submarines

The problem with the diesel-electric engine was that a full battery lasted no more than two hours at top speed. This severely limited the usefulness of submarines against the more powerful surface carriers and warships. This changed with the invention of yet another *Nautilus* in 1954, which became the first nuclear-powered submarine. Invented in the US, it needed only a very small amount of a nuclear fuel called uranium. But with this small quantity, it could stay underwater and move at high speeds for as long as needed. Amazingly, the speed was still created by steam-driven turbines; only the fuel was no longer oil, coal, or electric battery.

▲ *Modern model of a submarine. These kinds of submarines are used by nations around the world*

▶ *Built in 1940, the V-80 used a turbine engine invented by German scientist Hellmuth Walter. It burned hydrogen peroxide—used in disinfectants and bleaches. This released oxygen instead of steam that propelled a turbine and powered the submarine*

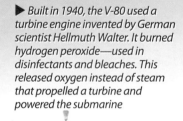

⊙ Incredible Individuals

German inventor Wilhelm Bauer (1822–1875) was a pioneer submarine-builder. During the coronation of Russia's Tsar Alexander II, Bauer took several musicians into his submarine at St Petersburg's Kronshtadt harbour. Once under water, they began playing the Russian national anthem, which was heard by people in ships across the harbour! Bauer's 52-foot iron submarine *The Marine Devil (Le Diable-Marin)* could carry 11 people and had windows, from which Bauer took what may be the world's first underwater photographs.

▲ *Coronation of Alexander II by Mihaly Zichy*

▼ *Gato- and Balao-class submarines were used in the US submarine campaign during the Pacific war*

(SS-383)

Flights of Fantasy

Human beings have wanted to fly like birds since time immemorial. Our myths and legends are full of heroes who found ways to fly, such as Icarus of Greece who flew too close to the Sun on wings of wax and feathers, or King Kaj Kaoos of Persia who harnessed eagles to his throne and flew over his kingdom. Even so real a figure as Alexander the Great is mythologised as flying in a basket pulled by gryphons!

🔍 A Timeline of Flight

The first person to design realistic flight was Leonardo da Vinci. In the late 15th century, he illustrated his theories of flight with the ornithopter. Since then, flying has come a long way.

💡 Isn't It Amazing!

> The modern conception of the aeroplane dates as far back as 1799. The concept was another of Sir George Cayley's achievements.

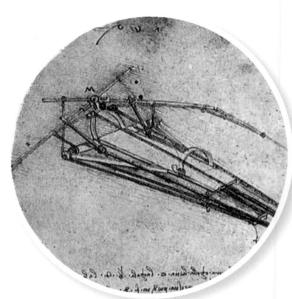

▶ *The ornithopter was never actually built, but da Vinci's concept can be seen in modern-day helicopters*

1783

The brothers Joseph and Jacques Montgolfier invent the first hot-air balloon. Its first live passengers are a sheep, a rooster, and a duck. A few months later, Pilatre de Rozier and Francois Laurent are its first human passengers.

▲ *Crowds watch the Montgolfier Balloon ascend from the Royal Estate of Aranjuez, Spain*

1804

English engineer Sir George Cayley successfully flies a model glider. In 1853, he sends his frightened coachman on the first manned glider flight!

▲ *George Cayley's glider*

★ Incredible Individuals

Amelia Earhart is one of the most inspiring aviators of all time. Even as a child, she was independent and adventurous. Earhart fell in love with flying in the 1920s. In 1928, she became the first woman to fly across the Atlantic Ocean. In 1931, she set the record for highest altitude reached in flight.

Throughout her life, Earhart's exploits captured the public's imagination. On 1 June 1937, she set off to fly around the world. Until 2 July she was recorded making regular fuel stops. But she was never seen again, after that day. A massive rescue party—the most expensive in American history until then—was launched to find her. It did not turn up with any clues. On 5 January 1939, Earhart was declared dead. An eternal celebrity, Amelia Earhart is the subject of many books, movies and plays.

▲ Amelia Earhart, one year before her fateful journey

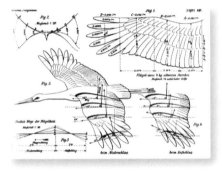

◀ Drawings from Lilienthal's book titled 'Bird Flight As The Basis Of Aviation'

1891

American scientist Samuel Langley successfully builds a model plane powered by a steam engine. However, when he tries to convert it into a full-sized plane, it turns out to be too heavy and crashes to the ground.

1896

After more than 2,500 flights, German engineer Otto Lilienthal is unfortunately killed in 1896, when his glider crashes due to strong winds. Lilienthal's pioneering book on aerodynamics is later used by the Wright brothers for their designs.

▲ Otto Lilienthal (1848–1896)

1903

The Flyer, built by brothers Orville and Wilbur Wright, lifts off at 10:35 am on 17 December. It weighs about 272 kilograms and is piloted by Orville. The brothers take turns to fly it. During the first flight that day, the Flyer covers about 120 feet in only 12 seconds.

▶ Markers at the Wright Brothers National Monument

END OF 1st FLIGHT
TIME: 12 SECONDS
DISTANCE: 120 FT
DEC. 17. 1903
PILOT: ORVILLE

Soaring High

The Wright brothers' Flyer is a biplane. This is a flying machine with two sets of wings, one above the other. Throughout WWI, this was the most popular model for planes. From the 1930s onwards, advancements such as stronger engines and better building materials led to improvements in the monoplane. These became the regular aeroplanes we see today. The conquest of the skies gave some countries a huge advantage over others. Over the 20th and 21st centuries, it led to fierce technological competition, which has given us some truly advanced planes.

▶ *The jet engine was invented around 1936–1937 in Great Britain, by Frank Whittle (1907–1996), and in Germany by Hans von Ohain (1911–1998). In 1939, the German-made Heinkel He 178 became the first jet plane*

▲ *One of the earliest iconic plane chases belongs to Alfred Hitchcock's suspense thriller North by Northwest, where actor Cary Grant is chased by a crop duster*

🔍 Crop Dusters

After WWI, people began to use old biplanes to fly over farms and spray pesticides. This process, called crop dusting, is still in use today—though not with biplanes anymore.

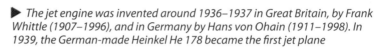

▲ *The largest airship ever built was the 245-metre-long German* **zeppelin**, *Hindenberg, which could carry over 1,000 people. In 1937, its hydrogen-filled balloon caught fire and crashed, killing 36 people. This marked the end of commercial zeppelins*

Manfred von Richthofen (1892–1918), or 'the Red Baron' was possibly Germany's top flying ace during WWI. He shot down some 80 enemy aircrafts, many of them from a German Fokker, which was a triplane. The Baron himself was killed while flying this plane on 21 April 1918.

💡 Isn't It Amazing!

On 14 October 2012, Felix Baumgartner jumped off a capsule on the edge of space , that is, 38.9 km high, with nothing to save him but a parachute. He became the first man to break the speed of sound in a free fall. His nail-biting nine-minute journey was watched that day by eight million people on YouTube!

The Harrier 'jump-jet' fighter-bomber is powered by a vectored thrust turbofan engine. This means that the engine can thrust downwards to push the plane vertically into the air. Thus, these Harrier jets do not need runways.

▼ *On 14 October 1947, the Bell X-1 became the first aircraft to exceed the speed of sound, reaching 1,126 kmph (or Mach 1.06). It was powered by a rocket engine and piloted by Captain Charles Yeager over the Mojave Desert, USA*

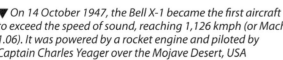

▲ *Felix Baumgartner, also holds the record for the world's lowest BASE jump*

Supersonic Passengers

The Douglas DC-8 was the first commercial plane to break the sound barrier. However, the most memorable has been the Concorde. It reached top speeds of 2,179 kmph (**Mach** 2.04), which allowed it to cross the Atlantic in 2 hours 52 minutes and 59 seconds. It started flying in the 1970s but turned out to be so noisy and expensive, it was shut down in 2003.

▼ The sleek Concorde

Around the World in Nine Days

In 1986, the Voyager became the first plane to fly non-stop around the world. Piloted by Dick Rutan and Jeana Yeager, the super-light aircraft was actually made using layers of carbon-fibre tape glued together and epoxy-saturated paper.

▲ Almost all parts of the Voyager's frame, including the wings, were filled with fuel which was four times heavier than the plane itself

When Cars Fly

The incredible Terrafugia Transition is a flying car! This small plane can fold up its wings in less than 30 seconds and turn into a car. It can then continue on the road and drive up to a regular petrol station if it needs to refuel. It is not yet on sale, as engineers continue to improve its technology.

The Transition can fly at speeds of 172 kmph and drive at a speed of 105 kmph. Do you think it will bring traffic jams to an end?

In Real Life

After 1969, international air travel became affordable with the invention and introduction of the Boeing 747. This was the first jet plane to have a wide body, seat 400 passengers, and still fly safely and speedily across large distances.

▲ Any plane carrying the President of the USA is called Air Force One. Since 1991, this name has belonged to a pair of specially outfitted Boeing 747 jets

Environment-friendly Planes

Modern planes are among the biggest gas guzzlers harming our planet. In 2003, Swiss pilot and engineer Adre Borschberg began the project Solar Impulse. Its aim was to develop a plane that ran on clean, renewable solar energy. This led to the invention of the Solar Impulse II in 2014. Running entirely on batteries powered by sunlight, it circumnavigated the globe in 2016. The non-stop flight was 118 hours long—that is almost five days!

▶ The Solar Impulse II in its hangar at Hawaii

The Rocket Launch

The invention of the rocket engine kicked off the exploration of the vast, mysterious universe. This remarkable engine is not the creation of any one person; rather, it came about over centuries through the hard work of many scientists. Notably, in the 17th century, Sir Isaac Newton gave us the three laws of motion, which form the basis for modern rocketry. Another key figure is Robert H. Goddard, whose lifelong research in rocketry led to many innovations. Among other things, he was the first person to use liquid fuel successfully to fly a rocket.

▶ *Newton's third law says that to every action there is an equal and opposite reaction. Rocket engines act by forcing hot gases downwards. This creates an equal force in the opposite direction, which causes the rocket to shoot upwards*

🔍 The Making of Missiles

Thought to be a Chinese idea, rockets themselves were first used as weapons several hundred years back. In 1232, flaming rockets destroyed a Mongol army besieging the Chinese city of Kaifeng. These missiles were most likely made of explosive gunpowder—another Chinese invention. In Europe, rockets were first used by Mongol raiders against an army of Christian knights at the 1241 Battle of Legnica, in Poland.

⊚ Incredible Individuals

As a 16-year-old, Robert Goddard read HG Wells's thrilling science-fiction novel *The War of the Worlds*. It inspired Goddard so much, he actually dreamed of building a machine that could fly to space. On 19 October 1899, he climbed a tree behind his house and "imagined how wonderful it would be to make some device which had even the possibility of ascending to Mars…" In his diary, he wrote, "Existence at last seemed very purposive." Today, Robert Goddard is considered the father of modern rocketry.

▲ *Duke Henry the Pious led 30,000 soldiers against Mongol raiders at the Battle of Legnica. He lost to a storm of Mongol arrows and rockets*

▶ *Goddard with his first rocket*

Missile Revival

Despite its initial success, the rocket missile was more or less forgotten by the 17th century. It was revived again in 18th century India by Hyder Ali, the ruler of Mysore. His rockets were made of metal cylinders, which could harness the power of the rocket and travel well over a kilometre. His son, Tipu Sultan used them successfully against the British in the famous battles at Shrirangapattana. This technology caught European interest and led to many rocket-propelled missiles being developed during the two World Wars. Over the 20th century, a number of other inventions were combined with rocket technology to give us the extremely sophisticated missiles of modern times.

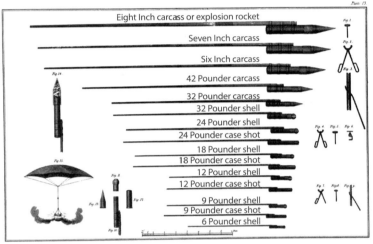

◀ Inspired by the rockets of Mysore, Englishman William Congreve experimented and designed better rockets, which were used in 19th century warfare

▲ Tipu Sultan, the Tiger of Mysore, had 5,000 rocket troops in his army. Their gunpowder came from Calcutta, which had one of the largest gunpowder factories of its time

An Accurate Missile

After Congreve's metal rockets, the next 19th century innovation in rocket technology came with British engineer William Hale's invention, the rotary rocket. This used jet vents to create spin, which made the rockets more stable and accurate—much like a bullet from a modern gun.

Getting off the Ground

If an object wants to escape Earth's gravity, it needs to shoot upwards at a speed exceeding 11.2 kmph. This is called escape velocity. During WWII, the Germans built the V2 missile, which became the first rocket capable of reaching space. After WWII, the Americans acquired the V2, fitted it with instruments and sent it to space. The rocket gave us the first real data about Earth's atmosphere.

▼ The V2 rocket was designed by Werner von Braun, a controversial pioneer of the Space Age

Reaching for the Stars

Space is a scary, unpredictable place for us earthlings. Things we take for granted, such as sunlight, heat, gravity, atmosphere, sound, and water are out there, but in warped and extreme forms.

Space science is still new and we are still discovering the rules of this alien environment. Institutes like NASA have large teams of scientists who work together to explore our universe. Some of their most basic research involves moving about in space. After all, if we cannot move, how will we ever begin our journey?

▲ *Yuri Gagarin, the first man to walk in space*

🔍 Man-made Satellites

Launched on 4 October 1957, Sputnik-1 was the first spaceship to successfully orbit the Earth. It moved on an elliptical path, completing its orbit every 96 minutes. In early 1958, it fell back towards Earth and burned up in the atmosphere. A month after Sputnik-1's launch, Sputnik-2 shot into space carrying the dog Laika, the first living creature to orbit the Earth.

◀ *Sputnik-1 was a little smaller than a basketball but weighed as much as an adult man*

👤✓ In Real Life

On 16 July 1969, the Apollo 11 space vehicle was launched on the Saturn V rocket. Once in space, the lunar landing module—carrying astronauts Neil Armstrong and Edwin "Buzz" Aldrin—broke away and made the first successful trip to the Moon.

🔍 Zero Gravity, Zero Atmosphere

On Earth, we are able to move by interacting with forces like gravity and air pressure. Space, however, is a near-vacuum. You can float weightlessly in it, but moving with precision is difficult. Large crafts can move using the rocket engine to thrust forward. But there is only so much rocket fuel you can carry into space.

The rocket engine is simply not fast enough to cover the enormous distances of our solar system—let alone our galaxy or the universe! Scientists are inventing new engines to solve this problem. Nuclear reactors and engines powered by plasma and magnets are some of the options.

▽ *On the Moon: lunar vehicles of a NASA expedition*

A Guide to Space Travel

The light year measures distance, not time. Light travels 300,000 km in one second. This means, it travels 9.5 trillion km in one year. This distance is called one light year. The closest stars to our Sun are Alpha Centauri A and Alpha Centauri B. They are about 4.3 light years from Earth.

The truly far-flung parts of the universe are measured in parsecs. One parsec is equal to 3.26 light years. Our galaxy, the Milky Way, is about 30 kilo-parsecs (100,000 light years) wide. The farthest star known to us is Icarus; it is about 15,330 mega-parsecs (50 billion light years) away.

▲ *Distances within our solar system are measured in Astronomical Units (AU). 1 AU is 149,598,000 km. This is the average distance between the Sun and Earth. The outermost planet, Neptune is 30.1 AU from the Sun*

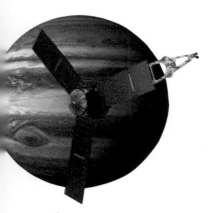

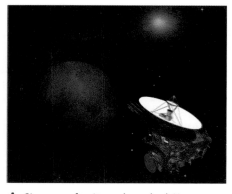

Space Stations

Another way to overcome the problem of moving through space is to build space stations that can refuel spaceships. Since 1971, some 11 space stations have successfully orbited our planet, most famously the International Space Station (ISS). Since 1981, scientists have also launched reusable crafts called space shuttles, some of which were used to build the ISS.

▲ *On 5 August 2011, the spaceship Juno began a journey to Jupiter, reaching five years later in July 2016*

▲ *Six years after it was launched, New Horizons flew to the edge of our solar system in July 2015, becoming the first spacecraft to explore Pluto and its five moons up close*

▼ *People have lived on the International Space Station since November 2000. It is as big as a house with five bedrooms, and even has two bathrooms, a gym and work spaces*

MEDICAL INVENTIONS

MEDICAL MARVELS

In ancient times, human beings believed that disease was not natural, but rather, a supernatural phenomenon. Diseases were thought to be the result of an enemy's curse or a sign of God's displeasure. They were even thought to signify that you were possessed by a demon. Thus, the earliest doctors were also sorcerers!

In the 5th century BCE, doctors began to set aside superstition and looked for physical causes of illnesses. Great leaps in medicine were made in the Middle East during the Middle Ages. Finally, in the 19th century, microorganisms like bacteria and viruses were identified as agents of disease. Since then, life-saving inventions in the medical field mark some of the most extraordinary achievements of humankind.

◀ Specialised teams of doctors and scientists have been the reason behind many medical miracles

A Peek Inside the Body

When doctors first began to look for natural causes of illnesses, they did not have the proper tools to help them. Devices like the thermometer and stethoscope had not been invented. So, doctors had to use their eyes and ears to observe patients and diagnose diseases.

Modern Medical Equipment

These days, medical experts have hi-tech imaging equipment that shows what is happening inside a patient's body. Such technologies include X-ray, ultrasound, and MRI. Other machines like the **EEG** and **ECG** chart our brain waves and heartbeats, so doctors can tell if they are functioning normally.

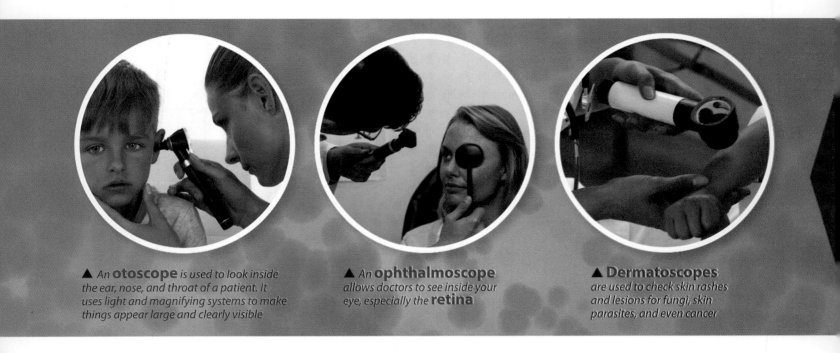

▲ An **otoscope** is used to look inside the ear, nose, and throat of a patient. It uses light and magnifying systems to make things appear large and clearly visible

▲ An **ophthalmoscope** allows doctors to see inside your eye, especially the **retina**

▲ **Dermatoscopes** are used to check skin rashes and lesions for fungi, skin parasites, and even cancer

Checking Your Temperature

When you feel ill, the first thing to do is to check if you have a fever. The tool with which you measure your body temperature is called a thermometer. The Italian mathematician Galileo Galilei invented the earliest known thermometer in 1592. The first accurate mercury thermometer was created in 1714 by German physicist Daniel Gabriel Fahrenheit. The Fahrenheit scale of temperature measurement, in which ice melts at 32° F and the temperature of a healthy human body is 96° F, was named after him. In 1742, Swedish astronomer Anders Celsius gave us the other popular scale, the centigrade or Celsius.

▲ A patient using a modern digital thermometer

◄ When heated, the air inside the glass tube of Galileo's thermometer expands, changing the level of the liquid. The glass bulbs carry temperature markers corresponding to the liquid

🔍 Isn't It Amazing!

Celsius originally used 0° C as the boiling point of water and 100° C as the melting point of snow. It was later turned around and became more popular with 0° C as the melting point of ice and 100° C the boiling point of water.

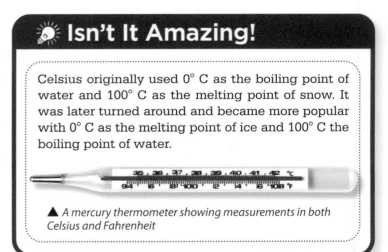

▲ A mercury thermometer showing measurements in both Celsius and Fahrenheit

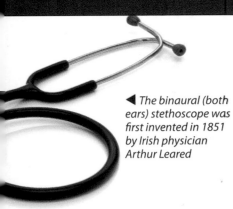

🔍 Listening to the Body

◀ *The binaural (both ears) stethoscope was first invented in 1851 by Irish physician Arthur Leared*

The first stethoscope was invented in 1816 by French physician Rene Theophile Hyacinthe Laennec. The stethoscope allows doctors to clearly listen to sounds within a patient's body. Most often, doctors listen to the sounds made by the heart and lungs using the stethoscope.

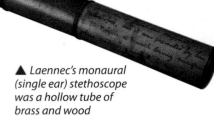

▲ *Laennec's monaural (single ear) stethoscope was a hollow tube of brass and wood*

🔍 Digital Thermometers

Nowadays, mercury thermometers are being replaced by digital models. Digital thermometers work by using a thermistor—a material whose resistance to electricity changes with changing temperatures. This resistance is measured by a computer chip inside the thermometer. The measurement is converted into a temperature reading, which is then shown to us on a display screen.

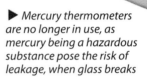

▶ *Mercury thermometers are no longer in use, as mercury being a hazardous substance pose the risk of leakage, when glass breaks*

🔍 Measuring Blood Pressure

A healthy heart is necessary for pumping blood throughout the body. When blood is pushed into blood vessels, it naturally presses against the walls of the vessels. This pressure is measured using a machine called a **sphygmomanometer**. Blood pressure can be affected by a huge number of illnesses. It is, therefore, one of the first things that doctors check to understand the state of your health. The first useful sphygmomanometer was invented by Austrian physician Karl Samuel Ritter von Basch in 1881.

An inflatable pad on the sphygmomanometer is wrapped around your upper arm and air is pumped through it, until it squeezes your arm. The doctor then measures your blood pressure using a stethoscope and the measuring counter attached to the sphygmomanometer.

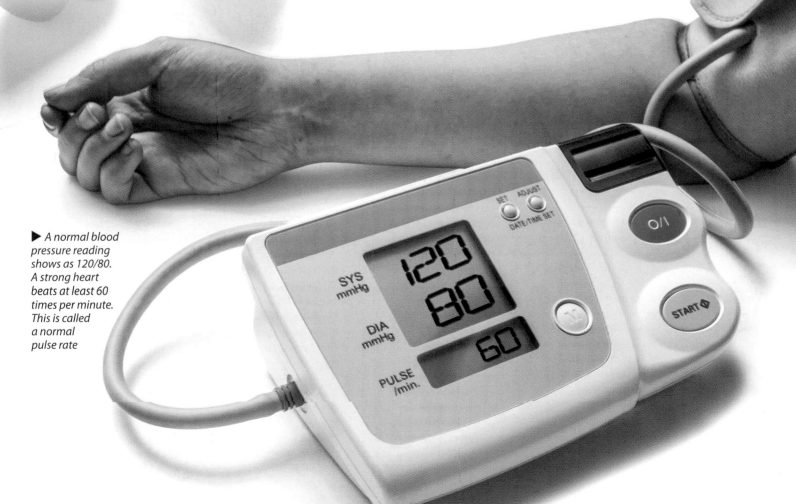

▶ *A normal blood pressure reading shows as 120/80. A strong heart beats at least 60 times per minute. This is called a normal pulse rate*

Photography for Physicians

Colours are made of electromagnetic rays called light. Apart from light, there are numerous other electromagnetic waves that are invisible to our eyes. Light cannot get in and out of our body, but certain sounds and electromagnetic waves can. Using these, inventors have built incredible machines to 'photograph' what is inside the body. Such imaging devices are used by doctors to diagnose your illness without cutting you open.

The Invisible X Factor

In 1895, German physicist Wilhelm Röntgen first discovered the presence of invisible **electromagnetic rays**. He called these mysterious waves X-rays. Unlike light, X-rays can pass through our bodies, but only through some parts. Bones and dense tissue are too thick for X-rays to penetrate.

If you put a piece of photographic film in the background, the X-rays that pass through the patient will hit the film and turn it black. The parts of the body that stop X-rays from going through will be outlined in white. Thus, X-ray photographs are used to look for damaged hard tissues, such as bone fractures.

▲ *This image shows a series of MRI scans of the brain from different angles*

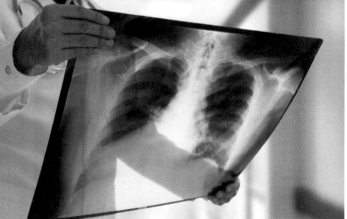

◀ *An X-ray film of the chest cavity; bones of the rib cage, spine and shoulders appear in white*

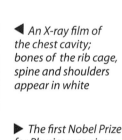

▶ *The first Nobel Prize for Physics was given to Röntgen in 1901, for his extraordinary discovery of invisible rays all around us. It ushered in a new era for physics and revolutionised medicine*

CT Scan

A Computed Tomography (CT) scan is a special type of X-ray machine. It was developed in the 1970s by Godfrey Newbold Hounsfield and Allan MacLeod Cormack, who shared a Nobel Prize for it in 1979. CT scans are popular in medicine for their detailed, high-resolution images. More importantly, they are able to photograph cross-sections of organs, so doctors can see what your organs look like from the inside.

⭐ Incredible Individuals

During WWII, a brilliant scientist named Marie Curie equipped vans with X-ray machines, so doctors could look for bullets inside wounded soldiers. The vans were fondly called 'petites Curies' (little Curies).

The Amazing MRI

Another Nobel-winning invention of the 1970s was Magnetic Resonance Imaging (MRI). This method gives high-contrast, 3D images of organs without using X-rays. Instead, it uses powerful magnetic fields about 1,000 times stronger than your fridge magnet.

The results are incredibly detailed images of soft tissues inside your body. Sir Peter Mansfield and Paul Lauterbur were the prize-winning minds behind MRI science. However, it was physician Raymond Damadian who invented the first full-body MRI scanner.

Isn't It Amazing!

It might seem strange now, but the idea for ultrasonography actually came from ships. Specifically, the idea for the ultrasound machine came from an instrument that was used to detect flaws in ships! In the 1950s, Scottish physician Ian Donald and engineer Tom Brown invented the ultrasound prototype for use in **obstetrics**.

▲ *During an MRI scan, the patient lies very still inside a large cylindrical machine that creates steady and strong magnetic fields*

Ultrasonography

Very high-pitched sounds are called ultrasounds. Some animals, like bats and whales, use ultrasound to visualise their surroundings! Likewise, doctors use ultrasound machines to look inside patients.

The machine sends ultrasound waves into the body. The sound that bounces back after hitting body tissue is called the echo. Different intensities of echoes are used by the machine to understand the relative position of tissues. This information is used to create an image of the tissues inside the body.

▶ *Unlike X-rays, there are no health risks associated with ultrasound. It is therefore used to check the health of a baby inside a mother's womb. CT scans and MRIs are also prohibited for pregnant women*

Testing Patients

Doctors often take blood and urine samples to diagnose deficiencies and infections in body tissue or fluids. Our blood may look red, but it is largely made up of a pale yellowish liquid called plasma. The red colour comes from red blood cells, which carry oxygen to different parts of our body. There are also white blood cells, which fight diseases, and platelets which form blood clots when we get hurt.

🔍 Why Take a Blood Test?

In a healthy body, all the elements of the blood, such as the white blood cells and red blood cells, are in balance. When the count of any one of them changes, it is a sure sign of illness. In particular, when your body is fighting a bacterial or viral infection, the number of white blood cells will show marked changes.

🔍 A Transport System

Blood vessels are like highways of the human body, transporting chemicals from one place to another. They carry nutrients from your gut (where food is digested) to the rest of the body. Therefore, blood tests for glucose, vitamins and minerals can show if your body is correctly absorbing nutrients from the food you eat. There are also hormones, which are special substances that affect your growth, emotions, energy, and other aspects of a normal life. Tests for these chemicals diagnose a wide range of serious illnesses, including the increasingly common condition, diabetes (related to the hormone insulin).

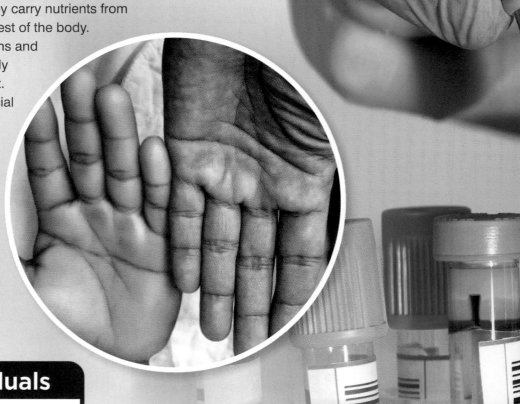

▶ *The most common ailment related to red blood cells is anaemia, where a person suffers from a deficiency of red blood cells or haemoglobin in the body. They may thus appear unhealthily pale or yellow*

⊛ Incredible Individuals

King Philippe-Auguste (1165–1223) of France had a doctor called Gilles de Corbeil, who described 20 different types of urine. A good teacher, de Corbeil turned his observations into *Poem on the Judgment of Urines*, so his students of medicine could memorise it all easily. The poem was popular for centuries.

Understanding Urine

On either side of our body, just where the ribcage ends, is a fist-sized organ called the kidney. The kidneys filter waste from the blood and send it out in the form of urine. At the same time, they ensure that things that are of use to the body, such as salts, water, and protein, go back into the blood. Most urine tests will, therefore, look for abnormal amounts of sugar, protein, **bilirubin**, blood cells, and foreign bodies like bacteria. This reflects the overall health of the blood, kidneys, and urinary tract.

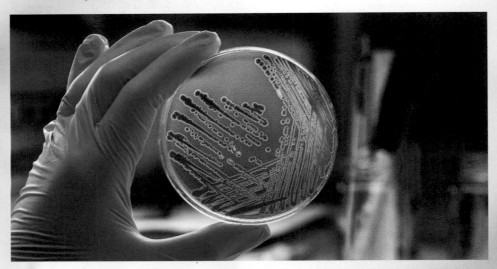

▲ *Urine culture refers to growing microorganisms present in urine in a petri dish, and it is used to check for abnormal bacteria. Gram-negative bacilli, seen here, are a group of bacteria responsible for many diseases including diarrhoea, cholera, plague, and typhoid*

In Real Life

There are many different kinds of blood tests. A Complete Blood Count (CBC) checks that you have the right proportion of cells in your blood. It can reflect disorders like anaemia, blood cancer and problems with your immunity or clotting mechanism. Other basic tests include Blood Enzyme Tests and Blood Chemistry Tests.

 # Testing Waste Matter

From a very early stage, human beings have been obsessed with checking, testing, and making notes on excrement. From such records, we know that the famously mad King George III of England may have suffered from **porphyria**, an illness that produces blue urine. However, the king was being treated with gentian at the time. So, it is also conjectured that the deep blue flowers of the plant might have given an unnatural colour to his urine.

Undeniably, waste matter from our bodies can reveal a great deal to our doctors. Thus, urine tests are a standard part of health check-ups in modern times.

The Need for Biopsy

To examine ailing organs, doctors may remove some sample tissue and observe it under a microscope. This is called a **biopsy**. The first biopsy to diagnose an illness was done in Russia in 1875 by M. M. Rudnev.

The simplest form of a biopsy today uses a needle to extract sample tissue. This is done for tissue that is just under your skin. More complex processes are involved in removing samples from deep within your body.

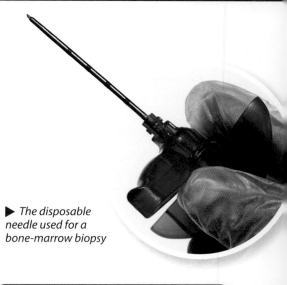

▶ *The disposable needle used for a bone-marrow biopsy*

🔍 The Syringe

The earliest known syringe-like device was used in Rome in the first century. During the 9ᵗʰ century CE, an Egyptian surgeon invented a suction syringe made of a hollow glass tube. It was only in 1946 that an all-glass syringe was invented. The hollow needle of the syringe was invented by Irish physician Francis Rynd. It was further refined by Charles Pravaz and Alexander Wood in 1853. In 1949, Australian Charles Rothauser created the first disposable plastic syringe.

👤✓ In Real Life

Hypodermic needles are an important invention as they are extremely hygienic and reduce chances of infection. The needle is so smooth that germs in the air do not get trapped on its surface. Also, the sharp needle creates a small puncture in your skin, which heals quickly, so germs cannot get in.

▼ *In a hospital, water, glucose, antibiotics, and other medicines are often sent directly to your blood by inserting a syringe in your arm and connecting it to the bottle of fluids with a tube. This is called Intravenous (IV) therapy*

▼ *Modern microscopes can send images of the tissue biopsy to computer screens for better visibility*

⊛ Incredible Individuals

Alexander Wood (1817–1884) used the hypodermic syringe to experiment with morphine, a drug that can relieve pain but, if taken in large doses, can also cause death. There is a rumour about him and his wife Rebecca Massey. It is said that the couple experimented by injecting morphine into their own bodies. They supposedly became addicted to the drug and the unfortunate Rebecca Massey became the first woman to die of a drug overdose from an injection. While this might just be a tale, it is true that many people had become addicted to morphine. In fact, during the American Civil War, addiction to morphine came to be known as the 'soldier's disease'.

🔍 Microscope

It is an invention that makes tiny objects appear large, so that they can be examined properly. The device consists of two or more lenses that can be adjusted accordingly for better clarity. The magnifying power of a microscope refers to how much it can visually enlarge an object. For instance, the notation '10x' means that the microscope can magnify an object to 10 times its original size.

▲ The handheld magnifying glass can show images that are 20 times (20x) larger than the original. A single-lens microscope can magnify up to 300x. Compound microscopes can magnify up to 2,000x

🔍 The Electron Microscope

Most microscopes use light to show enlarged images. The electron microscope (EM) uses a beam of electrons to do the same. Since electrons cannot travel far in the air, an EM requires airless space (vacuum) to function properly. This is well worth the trouble, as the magnifying power of EMs is extremely high (about 1000,000x).

▶ Images from a microscope can be photographed using a method called **photomicrography**

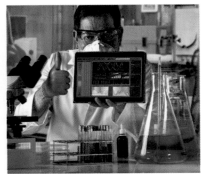

🔍 Inventing the EM

In 1931, Max Knoll and Ernst Ruska—both electrical engineers—built the first EM. It was a two-lens microscope that directly photographed the source of the electrons. Two years later, another EM took the first enlarged picture of an object. Finally, in 1935, Knoll was able to scan a solid surface using an EM.

▶ A researcher using a modern electronic microscope

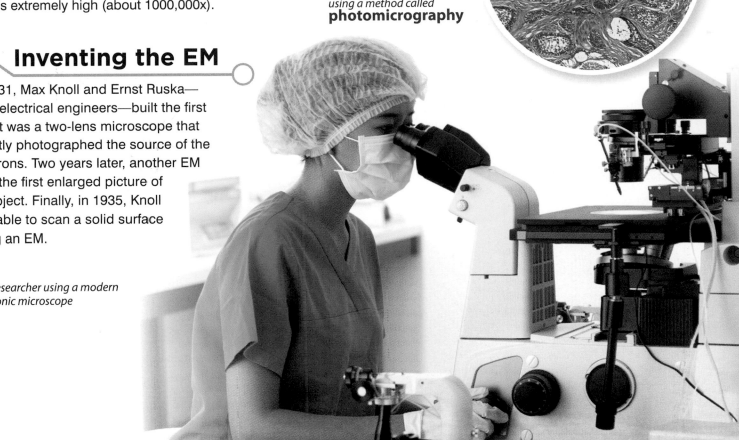
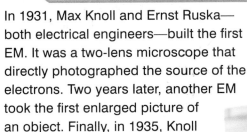

A History of Hygiene

In Greek mythology, Hygeia is the Goddess of health and the daughter of Aesculapius, the God of medicine. Although ancient civilisations did not know about germs, they understood that cleanliness and hygiene are linked to health.

A Timeline on Sanitation

Human beings of the very first civilisations (such as Indus Valley and Mesopotamia) were already building sewage systems, in order to dispose of waste in a safe manner. Of course, once the **germ theory** of the 19th century took root, doctors and governments worked hard to put strong hygiene practices in place.

2nd millennium BCE

Toilets are used in India, China, and other parts of the world. These are different from modern toilets.

1550–1200 BCE

Egyptians mix oils and salts to form a type of soap used to cure skin diseases.

3rd millennium BCE

Sanitation networks are made using brick and clay pipes to take sewage outside the cities. Medicinal sticks from certain trees are used to clean teeth. In ancient Rome, the rich pay to obtain clean drinking water.

2800 BCE

Soap-like products are seen in ancient Babylon.

▶ *The Indus Valley residents used bathing centres, wells, and water reserves to ensure hygiene*

In Real Life

King James VI of Scotland (1473–1513) was an energetic man who unified his country and made it wealthy. He was not particularly hygienic though. He did not take bath, believing it was bad for health. In fact, he wore the same clothes for months and even slept in them sometimes.

▲ *King James VI authorised the translation of the King James Bible*

Isn't It Amazing!

Romans thought that urine was an excellent stain remover and even used it as a teeth whitener at one point. Even during medieval times, people used a mixture of ashes and urine (called chamber lye) to clean clothes.

1498 BCE

The first bristle toothbrush is used in China. It is made of a bamboo handle with hair from a hog's neck.

▲ This toothbrush made for Napoleon Bonaparte dates back to 1795

600 BCE

Greeks begin using public baths and chamber pots (non-flushing toilets).

Incredible Individuals

A doctor called Ignaz Semmelweis discovered that his students were handling corpses and births at the same time. He insisted that the students wash their hands after tending to dead bodies. Within three months, deaths of newborn babies and their mothers had dropped by 20 times!

▲ A statue of Semmelweis in front of a hospital in Hungary

400 CE

In Britain, people begin using vinegar, mint and water as mouthwash. A concoction of bay leaves in orange flower water is also used for this purpose.

300 BCE

Rich Romans begin using wool and rosewater to wipe their bottoms. A century later, common people use sponges soaked in saltwater.

851 CE

Toilet paper is invented in China.

1819

A system that allows a toilet to flush properly is built. Unfortunately, it cannot be used due to a lack of running water.

1846

Britain faces a scarcity of firewood. As a result, hot baths become very expensive. Families and friends begin sharing bathwater or simply remain dirty.

18th century CE

The first dental chairs and dentures are invented. The latter consist of gold crowns and porcelain teeth. In 1790, a foot engine that rotates a drill for cleaning cavities is invented.

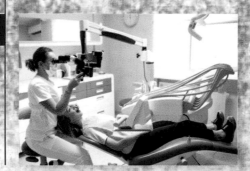

1861

The modern flushing toilet comes into use.

Preventing Infections

Most diseases that spread from person to person are caused by bacteria and viruses. If the infection is not too serious, our bodies are able to create chemicals called antibodies that fight off the disease. But wouldn't it be great if we had antibodies even before the infection? Then, the disease would not affect us at all.

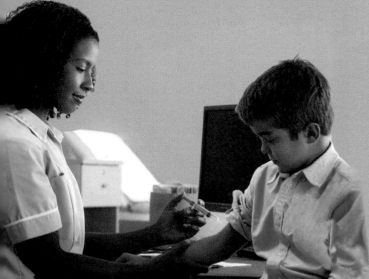

🔍 The Miracle of Vaccination

Vaccines are made up of weak or dead bacteria and viruses. They trick our body into thinking that it is being infected. The body then starts producing protective antibodies, even though we are not really ill.

Before vaccines, people used **variolation** (or inoculation) to prevent infections. This was done by applying old scabs or pus from infected boils on to a healthy person. The body responded by producing antibodies.

1000–1700 CE

Records from this time describe how people in China and India inoculated against the smallpox virus.

1796

Edward Jenner inoculates eight-year-old James Phipps with cowpox, a mild virus that spreads from cows to people. This breakthrough technique protects Phipps from the deadly smallpox virus. Jenner thus introduces vaccines to the world.

1805

Napoleon Bonaparte's sister Maria Anna Elisa Bonaparte becomes the first ruler to try to make vaccination mandatory. However, her initiative fails due to a lack of feasible methods to make the vaccination process compulsory.

1884

Louis Pasteur creates a vaccine that protects dogs from the fatal rabies virus. The following year, he saves a badly bitten nine-year-old boy named Joseph Meister, with a course of 13 rabies injections.

1885

Pasteur's student Jaime Ferran develops the first anti-cholera vaccine. During a cholera epidemic in Spain, he undertakes the first mass vaccination of some 50,000 people.

▼ An illustration of Dr Edward Jenner injecting young James Phipps with the cowpox virus

▲ Maria Anna Elisa Bonaparte (1777–1820)

▲ Louis Pasteur

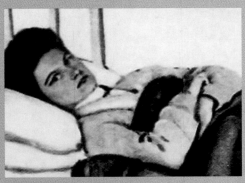

▲ An American maid named Mary Mallon became infamous as 'Typhoid Mary' in the 19th century. She knew she was ill, but continued to work at various households due to ignorance. By the time she was diagnosed, at least 51 people had been infected

⭐ Incredible Individuals

In 1661, China's Emperor Kangxi came to power when his father died of smallpox. Emperor Kangxi himself had survived the disease as a child. Therefore, he had his sons and daughters inoculated against the disease. The successful procedures made him a firm supporter of the practice.

▶ The Qing Dynasty's fourth ruler, Emperor Kangxi

1890s

British bacteriologist Sir Almroth Edward Wright invents an effective vaccine against typhoid. In 1899, the British army tests it on 3,000 soldiers in India during the Second Boer War.

1921

After 13 years of research, French scientists Albert Calmette and Camille Guerin develop the tuberculosis vaccine, calling it BCG (Bacillus Calmette-Guerin).

1936

Max Theiler creates the Yellow Fever vaccine, for which he later receives the Nobel Prize, becoming the only person to win the prize for the invention of a virus vaccine.

1938

Jonas Salk and Thomas Francis invent the first vaccine against influenza. It is used to protect US armed forces during WWII.

1939

American duo Pearl Kendrick and Grace Eldering develop the first effective vaccine for the deadly whooping cough.

1955

Jonas Salk's polio injection is approved. It is replaced in the 60s by an oral vaccine created by Albert Sabin.

1963

Dr John Enders and his team develop a safe measles vaccine.

2005

Measles, mumps, rubella and varicella are now combated using a single MMRV vaccine.

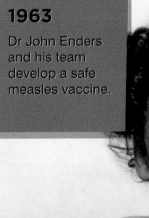

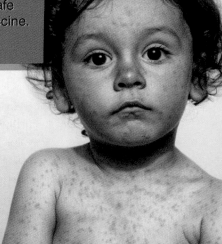

▶ A boy infected with measles

▲ The horse-drawn ambulance used during the last Yellow Fever epidemic in New Orleans, USA

An Infectious Theory

Antibiotics are chemicals produced by living creatures, which can affect the growth of other microorganisms. The chemicals are used to kill disease-causing microorganisms like bacteria. Before their invention, a great many people died from badly infected wounds. Even after bacteria were discovered in the 17th century, many doctors did not believe in their ability to cause infections.

Finally, in the 19th century, people were convinced that infections were caused by invisibly small organisms. The three heroes responsible for this achievement were Louis Pasteur, English surgeon Joseph Lister, and German physician Robert Koch.

▼ *Salmonella is a group of rod-shaped bacteria that cause many types of diseases, notably typhoid and food poisoning*

💡 Isn't It Amazing!

Although we think of microbes as harmful creatures, our bodies survive by hosting a wide variety of microbes. For instance, without a healthy population of bacteria in our gut, we wouldn't be able to digest our food properly. Many scientists now believe that being obsessively hygienic destroys good microbes and leads to issues like asthma, skin conditions, and allergies.

◀ *The greenish mould (a fungus) penicillium produces the invaluable antibiotic penicillin*

▲ *The Human Immunodeficiency Virus (HIV) is one of the deadliest viral diseases, as it takes away the body's ability to protect itself*

🔍 From Stale to Sterile: Penicillin

Antibiotics gained prominence during the 1940s, thanks to penicillin taken from the fungus penicillium. This powerful antibiotic was popularised by Alexander Fleming, Howard Florey, and Ernst Chain. All three shared a Nobel Prize for it in 1945. However, penicillin was neither the first antibiotic to be discovered, nor was Fleming the first person to discover penicillin.

🔍 Alexander Fleming

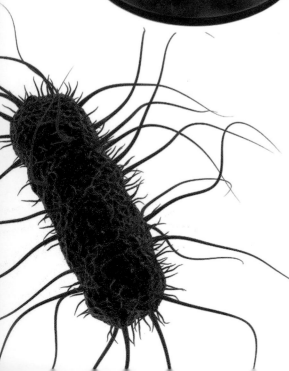

After he returned from a long holiday, Fleming set about clearing out some petri dishes in his lab. The dishes contained colonies of a deadly bacteria called *staphylococcus*. Somehow, a fungal mould had entered the bacterial culture. Fleming noticed that the mould was producing a 'juice' that was killing the bacteria. He got his assistants to isolate this liquid and studied its properties. It turned out to be the antibiotic penicillin.

A History of Antibiotics

Though they did not know about bacteria, people in ancient Egypt, China, Greece, and Rome knew how to use antibiotics. They used mouldy bread (which releases antibiotic chemicals) to treat infected wounds.

In the 19th century, Rudolf Emmerich and Oscar Low isolated pyocyanase from a green bacterium found in injured people's bandages. When this antibiotic was used in hospitals, different patients displayed different reactions and some even felt no difference.

In 1909, German physician Paul Ehrlich discovered the chemical arsphenamine, a successful cure for adults affected by the syphilis bacteria. Arsphenamine became the predecessor of the modern antibiotic.

▲ *Paul Ehrlich in his lab*

Incredible Individuals

Most schools teach us that penicillin was discovered in 1928 by Alexander Fleming. But this may not be true. In 1870, Sir John Scott Burdon-Sanderson noted that certain types of mould stopped bacteria from growing. Soon after, Joseph Lister experimented on penicillium and proved its anti-bacterial effect on human tissue. In 1875, John Tyndall also presented his experiments with penicillium. Most importantly, in 1897, Ernest Duchesne saw Arab stable boys applying mould from horse saddles on to their own saddle sores as a cure. He found that this mould was indeed penicillium and used it to successfully cure typhoid fever in guinea pigs.

▲ *Louis Pasteur had 5 children, sadly he lost 3 of them to typhoid*

The Works of Louis Pasteur

Little was known about microorganisms in the early 19th century. It was French chemist and microbiologist Louis Pasteur (1822–1895) who proved that germs were living beings. He discovered that milk turned sour because of microbes like bacteria. Further, heating milk killed the bacteria and made it safer to drink. This process is called pasteurisation. It is now a standard practice for many foods and drinks. Pasteur's idea also led to the boiling of instruments before surgery, to rid them of infectious bacteria. Most importantly, his work led to the development of vaccines against infectious diseases.

Indispensable Medicine

The 20th century saw groundbreaking advances in the invention of medicines. As a result, the average human life is much improved and the human lifespan is steadily increasing. We live longer, healthier lives thanks to the medicinal marvels of the 20th century.

Allergies

When foreign substances enter our body, our immune system responds in a variety of ways to remove them. A strong immune system thus protects us from parasites and microbes. But sometimes, harmless bits of fluff may enter our bodies and cause the system to react. This unnecessary response is called an allergy.

Common things that cause allergies include pollen from flowers, dust, pet hair, insect bites, and even some foods like peanuts and shellfish. The term allergy was coined in 1905 by Austrian physician Clemens von Pirquet.

Incredible Individuals

Clemens von Pirquet was an Austrian physician. He invented a test for tuberculosis. In this test, a drop of a bacterial protein called tuberculin is scratched on to the surface of the skin. If the area becomes red and raised, it confirms that the person is infected with tuberculosis. In 1909, he showed that more than 90 per cent of the Viennese children he had tested were infected by the disease by the age of 14.

Pirquet also discovered serum sickness, a mild allergic reaction to an injection of serum. This eventually led him to coin and define the term 'allergy'.

▲ People can take tests to find out what they might be allergic to

Tackling Allergies

Allergies have existed since ancient times, affecting rich and poor alike. Famously, the Roman emperor Claudius was terribly allergic to his own horse! Allergies can be as mild as a bout of sneezing and deadly enough to cause shock and death.

Unfortunately, we are yet to find a permanent cure for allergies. However, it is easy enough to control them by using medicines called anti-allergens. These range from injections to ointments, tablets, and inhalers. Mild anti-allergens like Benadryl (used for hay fever, hives, and motion sickness) are easily available at pharmacies.

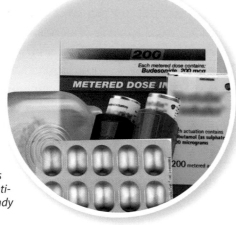

▶ People suffering from allergies must keep anti-allergens handy

Pain Relief

Any drug that takes away your pain without putting you instantly to sleep is called an **analgesic**. The best-known analgesic is aspirin. It is used to reduce fever and inflammation, and to remove aches in your muscles, joints, or head.

Aspirin is made from salicylic acid, a chemical that can be acquired from lots of herbs, fruits, grains, and even the bark of the willow tree. Clay tablets left by people from 4,000 years ago show that willow bark was used for pain relief. It has been a popular part of herbal medicine ever since. But it was only in the 19th century that salicylic acid was manufactured separately as a medicine.

▲ Modern aspirin was made by the chemical researcher Arthur Eichengrun. The first tablet appeared in 1900 and rapidly became popular in this form

Arthur Eichengrun

▲ Arthur Eichengrun (1867–1949)

Arthur Eichengrun was a Jewish chemist from Germany, known for developing a medicine called Protagol to cure gonorrhoea. The drug fell out of use after more successful antibiotics entered the market. Eichengrun also contributed to the study of plastics and their use, and to the creation of injections.

Eichengrun was a brilliant chemist and material scientist. But his claim to the invention of aspirin was denied due to the prevailing bias against Jewish people. The credit was given to another scientist for several years, until in 1999, when the other disputed claims were closely scrutinised and proven false. Eichengrun was once again credited with the invention of aspirin.

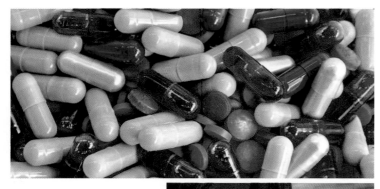

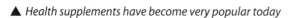

▲ Health supplements have become very popular today

In Real Life

Many over-the-counter (OTC) supplements are considered to be marketing gimmicks. There is not enough research to support their health benefits. Do not buy medicines without a doctor's prescription. Always read the labels carefully to confirm that you are buying the correct medication.

Health Supplements

Products such as multivitamin tablets, fish oil, probiotic drinks, and certain energy drinks are known as health supplements. Some vitamin and mineral tablets are also used as medicines. For instance, pregnant women in Asian countries are often given iron supplements to combat anaemia. Many people lack Vitamin D and take it in the form of supplements. Doctors also prescribe vitamin supplements to go along with antibiotics. This is because strong antibiotics can harm healthy cells and the vitamins help in restoration.

Sussing out Surgery

Often, acute injuries and illnesses cannot be treated by simply taking medicines. In such cases, doctors may open the affected part of the body and physically set things right.

Specially trained doctors called surgeons operate in specially equipped rooms called Operation Rooms (OR). They work under sanitised conditions to repair any damage or remove infected parts from inside the body.

In Real Life

During a heart attack, a person's heart stops beating. To revive it, doctors send an electric shock through the heart using a device called the defibrillator.

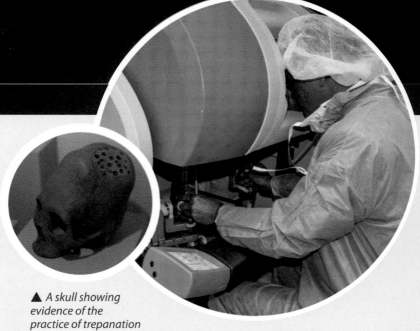

6500–3000 BCE
A form of surgery called trepanation (drilling a hole in the skull) is done by ancient humans in France. The purpose of this procedure is not yet known.

▲ *A skull showing evidence of the practice of trepanation*

◀ *Many modern surgeries are performed by robot arms, which are controlled by a surgeon using a computer. This helps doctors perform very precise and delicate operations.*

335–280 BCE
Alexandrian physician Herophilus **dissects** human cadavers in public. He is known as the 'father of **anatomy**'.

1452–1519
The multitalented Leonardo da Vinci dissects and draws human bodies with stupendous accuracy.

1792
Napoleon Bonaparte's military surgeon Dominique-Jean Larrey creates an ambulance service for soldiers on the battlefield.

1818
In Britain, James Blundell performs the first successful transfusion of human blood. He transfers blood from a husband to his wife, soon after childbirth.

1728–1793
British surgeon John Hunter carries out groundbreaking studies in human biology. He is called the 'father of modern surgery'.

1735
The first known **appendectomy** takes place.

▲ *Larrey's Flying Ambulances would take wounded soldiers to field hospitals, located a few kilometres away from the battle. Before this invention, injured men were simply left on the field until the battle ended*

▶ *Type AB Plasma can be transfused to people of all other blood types, but it is short in supply*

Isn't It Amazing!

Many ancient cultures, like India, China, and Egypt were familiar with surgery. However, in medieval Europe, surgery was done by barbers rather than doctors! In 1540, the United Company of Barber Surgeons of London was set up to finally bring some standards and training to the profession.

◀ *A painting depicting dentistry by a fashionable dentist in 17th century*

Timeline

1843
Ether is used as an **anaesthetic** for the first time. Four years later, James Simpson uses chloroform as an anaesthetic.

1865
British surgeon Joseph Lister discovers the use of antiseptics in surgery.

1893
The first successful open-heart surgery is performed in the USA, for a wound extremely close to the heart. Three years later, the first successful heart surgery is completed in Germany to repair a stab wound.

1905
The cornea of the eye is transplanted for the first time.

1940
A metal hip replaces bone for the first time.

1937
Blood banks come into being. They aid quicker blood transfusions.

1930
In Germany, a man undergoes an operation to become a woman named Lili Elbe.

1954
A whole organ (a kidney) is transplanted from one body into another. The patient lives on for eight more years.

2008
A laser is used in minimalist keyhole surgery to treat brain cancer.

2013
A successful nerve transfer allows a patient to move their formerly paralysed hand.

Incredible Individuals

Born in 1797, Dr James Barry was actually a woman who lived her whole life as a man, because women were not allowed to become surgeons. Dr James Barry became a British military surgeon and, upon her death, was buried as a man.

▶ *Barry's real name was Margaret Ann Bulkley*

Tumours: Benign and Malignant

Our bodies are made of tiny individual units called cells. Healthy cells are able to divide and produce new cells. However, uncontrolled cell growth produces extra lumps of tissue called tumours. Many tumours are benign, that is, they are not presently cancerous and do not spread throughout the body. They can usually be removed by surgery or shrunk using medical procedures. But when tumours continue to grow unchecked and start spreading to other parts of your body, they become dangerous. Such malignant growth is called cancer.

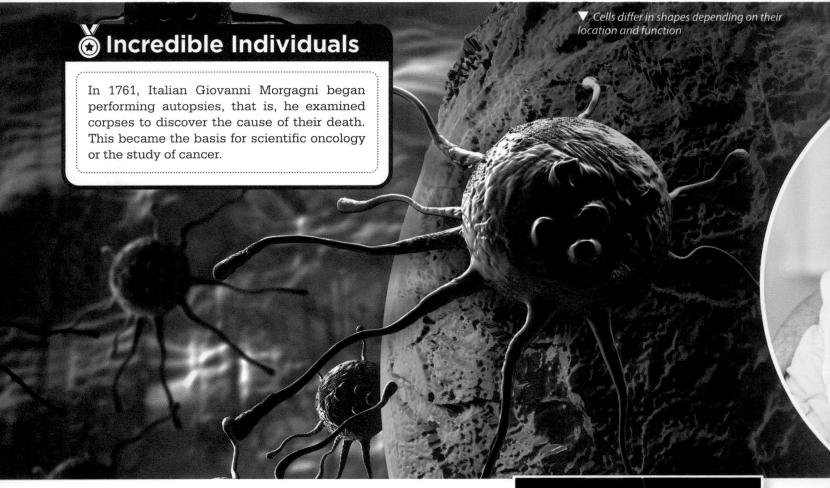

▼ *Cells differ in shapes depending on their location and function*

⊛ Incredible Individuals

In 1761, Italian Giovanni Morgagni began performing autopsies, that is, he examined corpses to discover the cause of their death. This became the basis for scientific oncology or the study of cancer.

🔍 Cancer Treatment

For most of human history, cancer was thought to be untreatable. This changed in the 19th century with the works of physicians Theodor Billroth, Sampson Handley, and William Halstead. Working independently, they discovered how cancers spread and how surgery could be used to successfully remove the ailing tissue.

Nowadays, surgical procedures are supported by other methods of cancer removal. In cryosurgery, liquid nitrogen (an extremely cold substance) is sprayed on abnormal cells to freeze and kill them. Sometimes, lasers are used to burn away the cancer. Yet another method places a small antenna inside the tumour. Radio waves are then sent to this receiver, which heats up and kills the cancer cells.

▶ *In Photodynamic Therapy, the patient is given a light-sensitive drug that can kill cancer cells. The doctor then shines a special type of light near the tumour. This activates the drug and destroys the abnormal tissue*

In Real Life

There are many reasons why healthy cells suddenly become cancerous. These include smoking, drinking alcohol, eating junk and foods containing saturated fat, lack of exercise, exposure to radiation, living in polluted air, and infection by certain viruses. On the other hand, eating fruits and vegetables can contribute in the fight to prevent cancer. In particular, broccoli and cauliflower have strong anti-cancer compounds.

▲ *A balanced diet and regular exercise lead to a healthy lifestyle, which helps prevent cancer*

Chemotherapy

During WWII, scientists in the US army discovered a compound called nitrogen mustard, which stopped a type of cancer. Soon after, American doctor Sidney Farber discovered aminopterin, a chemical that is similar to Vitamin B9 (folic acid). He found that this chemical worked against blood cancer in children. This became the first step in identifying more drugs that could be used against cancer. The use of such chemicals is called chemotherapy.

In the 20th century, doctors would first remove cancers through surgery. Then, radiation would be applied to control growths that could not be operated on. Finally, chemotherapy would be used to kill tumours that could not be removed through surgery or radiation.

Immunotherapy

Doctors are studying vaccines that help our natural immune system remove cancer. In 2018, the Nobel Prize for Medicine was awarded to James P. Allison and Tasuku Honjo, for their work in this field. Unlike other vaccines, which are given before an infection, some cancer vaccines are given after the disease is diagnosed.

▲ *While destroying cancer, chemotherapy also affects healthy cells. As a result, some patients experience hair loss, vomiting, diarrhoea, and anaemia*

▲ *Allison was born in Alice, Texas in the United States. He studied at the University of Texas in Austin and received his PhD in 1973*

▲ *Dr Tasuku Honjo was born in Kyoto, Japan. He studied medicine at Kyoto University and received his PhD in 1975*

Creating Living Tissue

It is fascinating to see living things' abilities and limits of regeneration. For instance, why can you regrow skin if you get a small wound, but not a whole arm if it gets cut off? There are other life forms whose regenerative abilities are much stronger than those of humans.

In Nature

Some lizards can regrow tails, sharks can make new teeth, and starfish can rebuild their entire body at times. In theory, if we had such regenerative powers, we could live very long, healthy lives. As a result, scientists have been trying to manufacture life in a lab for a very long time.

▶ In 1996, the sheep Dolly became the first mammal to be created in a lab. She was made using a cell from a ewe. She is, therefore, a clone (a copy) of her 'mother' and has no father

▲ At the centre of a cell is the nucleus, which is its command centre. When a cell divides into two, the nucleus produces a full copy of itself so that each new cell ends with one complete nucleus

Creation and Regrowth

With the discovery of cells, scientists began to get a clearer idea of how bodies heal and grow. In 1907, American scientist Ross Granville Harrison grew embryonic frog cells in a lab. This was the first-ever lab cultivation of biological tissue! But it was not until 1981 that tissue culture was used in practical medicine. This happened when biologists from the Eugene Bell Centre for Regenerative Biology and Tissue Engineering repaired wounds using artificial skin made from the patient's own cells. During the 80s, developing biological structures to replace damaged body parts came to be known as tissue engineering.

⊛ Incredible Individuals

Thomas Hunt Morgan (1866–1945) studied evolution, genetics, and embryology. He worked with fruit flies to show how genetic traits like eye colour are inherited through chromosomes, which is the name for the structures within a cell's nucleus. For his amazing discoveries in genetics, he won a Nobel Prize in **Physiology** or Medicine.

🔍 Stem Cells

In 1963, two Canadian scientists named James Till and Ernest McCulloch discovered a new type of cell in the bone marrow of mice. These came to be known as **stem cells**. Stem cells are unique because they can grow into any other type of cell in the body.

In Till and McCulloch's mice, the stem cells grew into different kinds of blood cells. Researchers are thus, interested in these cells because they can be used to replace damaged or dying tissues in the body. They are being studied for diseases that affect the brain, the heart, and many other organs. In 2010, a person with a spinal cord injury became the first to receive embryonic stem-cell treatment.

▲ *The Mexican axolotl is a salamander that can regrow parts of its brain, heart, lower jaw, tail, and missing limbs*

🔍 3D Bioprinting

In 1983, engineer Chuck Hull built a machine that could print physical objects. Instead of ink, it used plastic-like strands to create objects that you could hold in your hand. By the late 90s, scientists were trying to use it to print human tissue.

In 1999, a bladder was successfully printed on a framework of the patient's own cells. In 2002, a small but functional kidney became the first complex organ to be printed. In 2010, a company called Organovo printed the first blood vessel. Doctors are even aiming to transplant a fully functional printed organ, in the near future.

▶ *In a famous talk in 2011, Dr Anthony Atala held out a kidney that was printed by a 3D printer. The machine used MRI photos of the patient's actual kidney to spray layer after layer of human cells and create a new kidney*

Medical Aid

A great number of medical inventions make daily life better for ailing and ageing people. These range from spectacles and hearing aids to more sophisticated inventions that regulate your heartbeat or clean your body's waste.

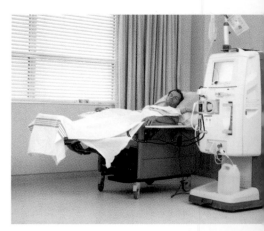

▶ A dialysis machine filters out waste from the blood of patients whose kidneys do not work. The first dialyser was invented in 1943 by Dutch doctor Willem Kolff

◀ The pacemaker uses electrical pulses to regulate heartbeats

Wheelchairs

Stone carvings from ancient China and paintings on Greek vases show people on wheeled devices. The earliest known wheelchair made specifically for a disabled person was in 1595. It belonged to King Phillip II of Spain.

In 1655, German watchmaker Steven Farffler made a self-propelled wheelchair for himself. Modern wheelchairs date from the 19th century. The first electric models were created by George Klein to help WWII veterans.

▶ In 1932, Harry Jennings, an engineer, built the first folding tubular steel wheel chair

Hearing Aids

A hearing aid is a gadget that amplifies the volume of sounds coming to the ear. Early hearing aids looked like trumpets. They had one wide end to collect as much sound as possible. The other, narrow end delivered sound into the ear.

The first electronic hearing aids were also very large. They had to be kept on tabletops and were not easy to move around with. They had large batteries which only lasted for a couple of hours. However, as technology advanced, the aids became small enough to fit inside the ear. Hearing aids today consist of a microphone, an amplifier (which increases the electrical current for a louder sound) and an earphone.

▲ Interestingly, both Alexander Graham Bell and Thomas Edison paved the way for hearing aids

Lenses

Lenses are curved pieces of transparent materials (like glass) that allow people to see more clearly. The first pair of modern spectacles—with two lenses and short arms going over the ears—was invented in the 18th century by an Englishman. Bifocals were developed around the same time.

The American leader Benjamin Franklin was among the first people to use bifocals. The first non-glass lenses were made of acrylic (a type of plastic) in the late 1940s. However, acrylic was not an ideal substitute for glass. It was only in 1962 that a proper lightweight, long-lasting plastic lens was manufactured.

▶ Before 1000 CE, monks used dome-shaped bits of magnifying glasses called reading stones to read texts

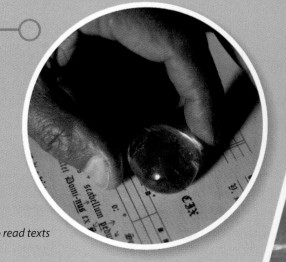

◀ The first wearable glasses were invented towards the end of the 13th century, most likely by an Italian. They were balanced on top of the nose

▼ Bifocals are lenses that are divided into two parts—the bottom part for long-sightedness (or hypermetropia) and the top part for near-sightedness (or myopia)

In Real Life

Nowadays, contact lenses are a popular alternative to spectacles. They were first conceptualised by Leonardo da Vinci. The first contact lenses were made from glass in 1887. Modern plastic contact lenses were first seen in the 1930s.

Artificial Limbs

The Roman general Marcus Sergius lost his right hand in the Second Punic War. He later replaced it with an iron hand, built to hold a shield so that he could continue fighting. This is one of the first known cases of a prosthetic (artificial) limb.

In the 16th century, French doctor Ambroise Paré invented hinged hands and locking knees. Modern prosthetics are also made of lighter, stronger materials like carbon polymers and plastics. Often, they are fitted with electronics that allow for better control over actions such as gripping, walking, jumping, etc.

▶ A prosthetic leg crafted for an athlete

▲ All prosthetic wears are custom made. Most of them are designed using titanium, aluminium, and carbon fibre

What is a Transplant?

In medicine, a transplant (or a graft) means taking tissue from its original location and using it to heal some other part of the body. It can be done with an entire organ or with some part of it. When a tissue is grafted from one part of your body to another part of your own body, it is called an autograft. Organ transplants are also made from one human being to another.

🔍 The History of Autograft

As far back as the sixth century BCE, surgeons in the Indian subcontinent were practising tissue grafts. Specifically, they could rebuild shattered noses using skin flaps from the patient's arm. The flap would remain attached to the arm until the nose area grew new blood vessels. After about two to three weeks, the arm would be freed from the nose.

This method spread to Western medicine in the 16th century through the efforts of Italian surgeon Gaspare Tagliacozzi.

▼ *The Sushruta Samhita, an ancient Indian text, outlines the process of skin grafts*

⊛ Incredible Individuals

Alexis Carrell developed groundbreaking ways to sew blood vessels together, for which he received the Nobel Prize in Medicine in 1912. His work laid the foundation for organ transplant surgery. In 1990, Joseph Murray received the Nobel Prize for his revolutionary work in advancing organ transplants using radiotherapy and immunosuppressants. He shared it with Donnall Thomas, who invented methods of providing bone marrow cells for transplant.

▶ *Alexis Carrell*

Transplant Successes

The body's immune system treats most transplants as foreign bodies and attacks them. All transplants—even autografts and transplants between identical twins—are prone to such rejection. To prevent this situation from arising, transplant recipients are given drugs called immunosuppressants, which help the body successfully cope with the transplant.

In the Western world, the first successful transplant was a skin graft performed in Denmark in 1870. It was not until 1954 that a whole organ, a kidney, was transplanted. Dr Joseph Murray, who performed the surgery on two identical twins, received a Nobel Prize in 1990.

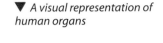

▼ *A visual representation of human organs*

Facts about Transplants

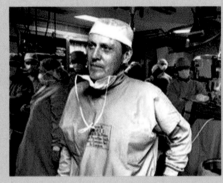

▲ *In 1969, Thomas Starzl performed a successful liver transplant. In the same year, Christiaan Barnard completed the first successful heart transplant*

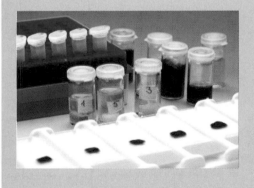

Before any transplant, samples of blood and tissue are taken from the donor and recipient. These are checked to see how well they match. Since 1977, computers have assisted in the organ-matching process. Many countries now keep state-wide or nation-wide systems of donor information.

In 1981, a combination heart-lung transplant was successfully executed by renowned surgeon Bruce Reitz.	In 1998, a full hand was successfully transplanted for the first time. The surgery was done in France.	A partial face transplant was also first successfully performed in France. Five years later, in 2010, a full-face transplant was achieved in Spain.

Genetics

Have you ever wondered why the biologically related members of a family look like each other? The answer lies in the nucleus of the cell. This dark nucleus is made up of microscopic matter called genes. The study of genes is called genetics. Genes give our cells their basic form and function.

Children inherit genes from their parents. Thus, they look like a mix of their parents, and can also resemble their siblings, grandparents, aunts, uncles, cousins, etc. Genes decide the colour of a flower, give the lion its mane, and differentiate a fish from a bird.

 ## DNA

Genes are made up of a chemical called deoxyribonucleic acid or DNA. Lots of DNA and protein come together to form thread-like structures called chromosomes. Different creatures have different number of chromosomes. A garden pea has 14 chromosomes and an elephant has 56. DNA itself has a peculiar shape called a double-helix. This was discovered by scientists Francis Crick and James Watson in the 1950s.

▶ *The double-helix DNA is formed by two entwined strands*

Human Genome Project (HGP)

A genome is the genetic make-up of an organism. Over 1990–2003, the Human Genome Project (HGP) identified and published all the thousands of genes that make up a human being. Going forward, this will help doctors and scientists understand how to improve human life, especially how to reverse ageing and cure inherited diseases.

⊛ Incredible Individuals

In 1962, Crick, Watson, and Maurice Wilkins won a Nobel Prize for discovering the structure of the DNA. However, they could not have done it without Rosalind Franklin's work. It was Franklin who obtained the images of DNA. She did so using X-ray techniques, which tragically led to her death by cancer. When the prize was awarded, Franklin—most unfairly—was left out!

 ▲ *Dr Francis Crick*

 ▲ *Dr James Watson*

 ▲ *Dr Maurice Wilkins*

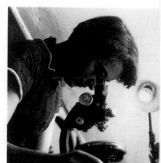 ▲ *Dr Rosalind Franklin*

Royal Rarities

Royalty has always considered itself special. In an effort to keep their blood 'pure', members of royal families often married their relatives. Eventually, they became so interrelated, new marriages were taking place between cousins. This is called inbreeding. It sometimes results in people being born with rare and tragic defects.

🔍 Haemophilia

The most infamous 'royal disease' was haemophilia. It occurs when blood clots do not form to stop a wound from bleeding. The illness affected many male descendants of Queen Victoria of England. She married her first cousin, Prince Albert. Their son Leopold fell and hurt himself. He died from blood loss. Through her daughters, haemophilia spread to other royal families of Europe. The two sons of the German Kaiser Wilhelm II, as well as the son of the Russian Tsar Nicholas II, were all haemophiliacs.

▲ After 16 generations of inbreeding, the royal Habsburg family of Europe started showing physical deformities. The Habsburg Jaw, seen here in Charles II of Spain, is the name for a jutting lower jaw—usually under a thick lower lip

🔍 Porphyria

Another disease of the blood, porphyria comes in different forms. James V of Scotland most likely passed it to his daughter Mary, Queen of Scots. She suffered from ulcers, mental illnesses, physical disablement and rheumatism since her teens. Her son James I of England had urine as 'purple as Alicante wine'—another sign of porphyria. Their descendent George III, nicknamed 'Mad' King George, would wander through the castle, blind, deaf and dirty. Unable to recognise anyone, he was sadly neglected by his caretakers. In 1810, his son forced his removal from the throne.

▲ A painting of George III of Great Britain commissioned during his younger, happier days

👤 In Real Life

King Henry VIII of England suffered from the very common disease, malaria. The first cure for malaria was found in South America. A feverish man, desperate with thirst, drank from a pool of water and was cured. He noticed that the water was bitter. It had been 'poisoned' by the surrounding cinchona trees. Over the 18th and 19th centuries, scientists found and purified the chemical from the tree. It is called quinine and is used to cure malaria to this day.

SPACE
DISCOVERIES

OUT IN **SPACE**

The earliest astronomers mapped the sky by observing it year after year. They discovered and named the nearest planets, moons, stars and shooting stars, and charted asteroids and galaxies. As our knowledge of the universe increased, scientists realised that all heavenly bodies followed certain rules.

Scientists used these observations, along with a pinch of imagination, and made calculations to decipher the universe. The study of the universe is called **cosmology** and the people who study it are called cosmologists. The study of the physical laws of the universe is called **astrophysics** ('astro' means stars). It is a pioneering branch of science that allows us to explore alien worlds.

▼ *Earth as seen from the Moon*

Cosmology:
From Ancient Times to the 19ᵗʰ Century

We have slowly but steadily managed to glean many secrets of the universe over the centuries. The course of cosmology has weathered the pressures of religion and superstition, the suppression of female scientists, the prejudices of class and race, and many other odds. Let us take a look at some of the most brilliant champions of this triumphant science.

Anaximander (610–546 BCE)

The first known person to develop a systematic view of the world was the Greek philosopher Anaximander. He was also the person who recognised that Earth moved freely through space. This idea may seem obvious to us now, but most civilisations of that time believed that the planet was upheld by pillars, heroes or beasts. So, he was quite a path-breaker at that time.

▲ *An ancient Roman mosaic depicting Anaximander holding a sundial*

◄ *A 1628 oil painting of the cheerful Democritus, by Dutch artist Hendrick Terbrugghen*

Democritus (460–370 BCE)

Democritus was also known as the 'laughing philosopher'. He believed that the universe was made of tiny particles called atoms. According to him, the universe contained infinite, diverse worlds that followed a set of physical laws rather than the whims of gods. He also worked out that the Milky Way's appearance was caused by the light of stars.

Aristarchus of Samos (310–230 BCE)

In ancient times, people thought Earth was at the centre of the universe. Mathematician Aristarchus first proposed that the Sun was at the centre of the universe. He proposed this model 18 centuries before Nicolaus Copernicus discovered the same.

▶ *A statue of Aristarchus at the Aristotle University of Thessaloniki, Greece*

▲ *Although not the first one to propose the theory, Nicolaus Copernicus (1473–1543) was the man who popularised heliocentrism, which theorises that the planets revolve around the Sun*

⊛ Incredible Individuals

Born a nobleman, Tycho Brahe (1546–1601) was kidnapped and brought up by his uncle. Brahe later refused to take his place at the royal court. Defying his family, he became a scientist. Brahe's work was revolutionary and brought new light to the understanding of planetary motion and gravity.

▶ A brilliant group of women known as 'Harvard's Computers' made significant contributions to astronomy. Among them were Henrietta Swan Leavitt (1868–1921), Annie Jump Cannon (1863–1941), Williamina Fleming (1857–1911), and Antonia Maury (1866–1952)

▼ The Kepler crater on the Moon is named in honour of Johannes Kepler

Hipparchus (190–120 BCE)

Hipparchus was one of the greatest Greek cosmologists. He was the first to accurately measure the distance between Earth and the Moon. His work revealed the existence of over 850 stars. He also discovered the 'wobbling' of Earth that causes the equinoxes. This is called **precession** and it was the third movement of Earth that was discovered after rotation and revolution.

◀ Almagest, written by Claudius Ptolemy (100–170 CE) was the ultimate guide to thousands of stars and constellations and to the movement of planets for 1500 years

Johannes Kepler (1571–1630)

Blessed with a keen intellect, Kepler propounded the laws of planetary motion. He also discovered that tides occur due to the gravitational pull of Moon. His work on planetary motion led Newton to discover the laws of gravity.

Isaac Newton (1643–1727)

Newton's laws of gravity and motion completely changed our understanding of physics and nature. Newton also invented the first reflecting telescope and showed how sunlight could be split into all the colours of the rainbow.

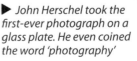

◀ Isaac Newton was a key figure of Europe's scientific revolution

John Herschel (1792–1871)

Nephew of the brilliant astronomer Caroline Herschel, John did the first global survey of stars. He built the first telescopic lab in the southern hemisphere and catalogued about 500 nebulae and over 3,000 double stars. He named seven of Saturn's moons and four of Uranus's moons.

▶ John Herschel took the first-ever photograph on a glass plate. He even coined the word 'photography'

The Space Race

The World War II ended in 1945. The US and Soviet Union had been allies during this war. But without a common enemy, the capitalist US and the communist Soviet Union soon turned against each other. Instead of clashing openly, they fought to establish their supremacy in various other fields of interest, such as race for outer space. This period is known as the Cold War.

🔍 The Space War

One of the few good things to come out of the Cold War was a spate of space-related technologies. In 1955, the US declared that it would launch a satellite into the outer space. The USSR decided to launch its own satellite first. Thus, began a fierce competition known as the space race.

▲ Taken at the height of the space race, this photograph shows Soviet leader Nikita Khrushchev with Valentina Tereshkova, the first woman in space and (in the far left) Yuri Gagarin, the first man in space. Between them is Pavel Popovich, another pioneering cosmonaut

1960

NASA launches the first successful weather satellite, Tiros-1. Its ability to detect cloud cover and predict hurricanes encouraged the development of the Nimbus programme of weather satellites.

29 July 1958

America establishes the National Aeronautics and Space Administration (NASA) after the success of Sputnik.

▲ NASA Headquarters in Washington D.C.

4 October 1957

The USSR becomes the first nation to successfully launch an artificial satellite. It is called Sputnik, a Russian word meaning fellow wanderer.

3 November 1957

A live animal, the dog Laika, orbits Earth for the first time on the USSR's satellite Sputnik-2.

1 February 1958

The US successfully launches a satellite called Explorer. It discovers the Van Allen radiation belt, which causes the polar lights called Aurora Borealis (in the Northern Hemisphere) and Aurora Australis (in the Southern Hemisphere).

◀ In 1958, TIME Magazine portrayed Soviet leader Nikita Khrushchev as the Man of the Year with the satellite Sputnik in his hands

◀ A statue of Laika in her space harness in Moscow, Russia

▶ The Aurora Borealis photographed over Norway

12 April 1961

The Soviets manage another first by launching the cosmonaut Yuri Gagarin into space.

◀ *Yuri Gagarin, the first man in space and the first to orbit Earth*

25 May 1961

US President John F Kennedy publicly commits the US to achieving the first human landing on the Moon.

◀ *US President John F Kennedy addressing Congress in 1961, announcing his ambitious goal of "landing a man on the Moon and returning him safely to Earth"*

16 June 1963

The Soviet Union launches Vostok-6 with Valentina Tereshkova, the first female cosmonaut to travel to outer space.

◀ *The first woman in space, Valentina Tereshkova, presenting a badge to the first man on the Moon, Neil Armstrong*

20 February 1962

NASA's 'human computers', an all-woman team of mathematicians, undertake mind-boggling calculations that give the US an edge in the space race. Katherine G Johnson's impressive mathematics skills help put American astronaut John Glenn into orbit around Earth.

◀ *Katherine G Johnson, whose calculations in orbital mechanics led to many successful missions, including the first Moon landing*

▲ *This USSR stamp from 1965 commemorates Leonov's historic walk in space*

20 July 1969

After a series of missions under the Apollo programme, the US spacecraft Apollo-11 lands on the Moon. Crew members Neil Armstrong and Buzz Aldrin spend 21 hours and 36 minutes on the Moon before successfully returning to the spacecraft. This brilliant achievement marks the end of the Cold War space race.

28 November 1964

The Mariner-4 explorer is launched. It becomes the first spacecraft to fly by Mars and send photographs and data about the planet.

18 March 1965

The Soviet cosmonaut Alexei Leonov becomes the first man to 'walk' in space. He leaves the spacecraft wearing an early spacesuit and walks in the vacuum of space for just over 12 minutes.

◀ *Buzz Aldrin on the Moon; reflected in his visor is Neil Armstrong taking the photograph*

Kicking off Space Exploration

Scientists have been working on fulfilling the human dream of space travel for centuries. During 1642–1727, Isaac Newton published his laws of motion and described gravity. This gave us a scientific basis for understanding rockets and orbits. Russian scientist Konstantin Tsiolkovsky (1857–1935) showed how rockets could be used to launch spacecrafts. He also calculated the minimum speed required to stay into the orbit around Earth. Finally, in 1942, the German aerospace engineer Werner von Braun and his team built V2, the first rocket to reach the boundaries of space, about 100 kms above Earth.

🔍 Rocket Development

A rocket is any weapon or vehicle propelled by a rocket engine. The medieval Chinese inventors of rockets used gunpowder for propulsion. Liquid-fuel rockets were developed by Robert H Goddard (1882–1945), the father of modern rocketry.

Modern ion rockets use solar-powered electricity to produce a stream of **ions**, which propel the rocket forward. The latest **plasma** rockets use radio waves to heat chemicals at such a high temperature that they turn to plasma (which is what the Sun is made of)! A powerful rocket like this could travel to Mars and back within a few weeks. But scientists have yet to figure out how to stop the rocket from melting in the heat it generates.

▼ US officials, including Werner von Braun, with a model Explorer-1, the first satellite launched by the USA into outer space.

👤✓ In Real Life

Many space exploration devices are launched on multi-stage rockets. These are made of two to five rockets, each of which carries its own engine and fuel.

▼ The evolution of Soviet space launch vehicles from the R-7 (the first-ever Intercontinental Ballistic Missile), the Sputnik launcher, the Vostok, the Voskhod launcher, and the Soyuz launcher

▶ India's PSLV, a four-stage launch vehicle with both solid-fuel and liquid-fuel rockets

R-7 (8K71)
Test vehicle
1957

8K71PS Sputnik
(PS) Launcher
1957

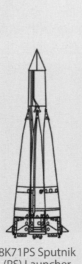

8 K72K Vostok
(3KA) Launcher
1960

11A57 Voskhod
(3KV) Launcher
1963

11A57 Soyuz
(7K-OK) Launcher
1966

Sputnik

Launched on an R-7 liquid-fuel rocket, the Soviet Union's Sputnik was the first artificial satellite to orbit Earth. It weighed 83.6 kilograms and travelled in an elliptical path above Earth for three months. At 29,000 kmph, it took 96.2 minutes to complete each orbit. After 1440 circuits, it burned up in Earth's atmosphere on 4 January 1958.

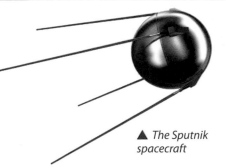

▲ *The Sputnik spacecraft*

A Cosmic Zoo

The first beings to go up in a rocket were most likely accidental passengers like bacteria or other microbes. In 1947, scientists sent up some fruit flies in a V2 rocket. They were given some corn to snack on during the trip. On 14 June 1949, Albert II became the first monkey to fly up in a rocket. He travelled 134 kilometres to the very beginning of space. Since then, 32 monkeys and a chimpanzee have journeyed to space. Several mice were launched during the 1950s. The dog Laika was the first animal to orbit Earth. Sputnik-5 was the first spacecraft to return with its passengers alive on 19 August 1960. These included 2 dogs, a rabbit, 42 mice, 2 rats, and fruit flies!

▲ *After some confused attempts, Arabella became the first spider to spin a web in space. Launched in 1972, Arabella and Anita were the first spiders in outer space*

◀ *The US launch of the V2 rocket carrying Albert II*

The First Spaceman

Flying the rocket Vostok-1, Yuri Gagarin (1934–1968) became the first man in outer space. From there, he was launched into orbit on the Vostok 3KA spacecraft, in which he successfully completed one orbit of the Earth. He famously whistled the tune of 'The Motherland hears, the Motherland knows, Where her son flies in the sky', a 1951 song by Dmitri Shostakovich. Awed by the sight before him, he reported to ground control, "The Earth is blue... How wonderful. It is amazing."

◀ *The Vostok-1 was notable for being the world's first space flight with a human on-board*

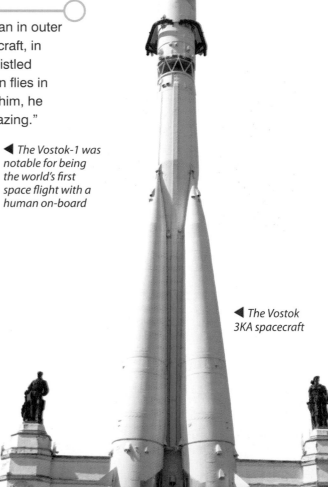

◀ *The Vostok 3KA spacecraft*

To the Moon and Back

In 1961, President John F Kennedy announced that the US would put men on the Moon before 1970. NASA achieved this goal when, on 20 July, 1969, the manned Apollo-11 spacecraft made a successful landing. Nearly 530 million people watched the event on live broadcast. Since then, there have been several missions to the Moon launched by the US, Russia, Japan, China, India, and Europe.

► *From left to right, this shows the Moon's near side, far side, north pole, and south pole*

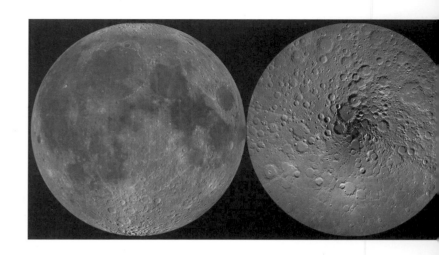

💡 Isn't It Amazing!

Just between the mid-60s and the mid-70s, there were some 65 Moon landings! However, only 6 Moon landings have carried human beings on board and only 12 people have ever walked on the Moon's cratered surface.

◄ *On 30 May 1966, the US robot spaceship Surveyor-1 reached the Moon. Its photographs gave NASA some vital information on how they might successfully land a crew of astronauts on the satellite*

🔍 The Dark Side of the Moon

The first human beings to orbit the Moon were the crew of Apollo-8. It comprised Frank Borman, James Lovell, and William Anders. The event occurred on 24 December 1968. While orbiting the Moon, they also became the first people ever, to see the dark side of the Earth's Moon.

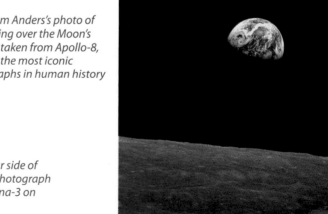

► *William Anders's photo of Earth rising over the Moon's horizon, taken from Apollo-8, is one of the most iconic photographs in human history*

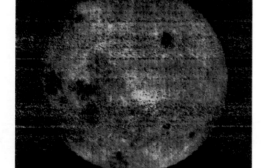

◄ *Our first view of the far side of the Moon came from a photograph taken by Soviet probe Luna-3 on 7 October 1959*

🔍 Man on the Moon

Apollo-11 launched on 16 July 1969. It carried Neil Armstrong, Michael Collins and Edwin 'Buzz' Aldrin. On 20 July Armstrong and Aldrin donned their spacesuits and climbed into a lunar landing module called Eagle, while Collins remained in orbit in the Columbia module.

The Eagle landed on a volcanic plain called Mare Tranquillity. Armstrong and Aldrin spent 21 hours and 36 minutes resting, exploring, and deploying experiments. Later, they re-joined Collins. On 24 July, Apollo-11 splashed down in the Pacific Ocean and the three astronauts were safely brought back home.

◀ *The Apollo-11 lunar crew (from left to right): Neil Armstrong, Michael Collins, and Buzz Aldrin*

▶ *The Eagle with its spidery landing pods and sensors, photographed in orbit by Columbia*

▶ *Apollo-11 lifting off on the three-stage, liquid-fuelled Saturn V rocket on 16 July 1969 from Kennedy Space Centre*

The Miraculous Apollo-13

Apollo-13 was meant to be the third manned mission to land on the Moon. But within two days of its journey, the oxygen tank in the service module failed, which ignited the damaged wire insulation. This caused an explosion which led to the relentless flow of oxygen in the outer space. The astronauts thought that they were doomed. Fortunately, NASA's scientists came up with prompt solutions using the limited equipment on board. They guided the astronauts to make the repairs and brought them home safely. The heroic story is celebrated in books, films, theatre, and even comics!

Lunar Road Trips

From 1971 onwards, American astronauts used a Moon car to explore the vast surface of Earth's satellite. This electric-powered vehicle, with a top speed of less than 13 kmph, was called the Lunar Rover. The Moon buggy made its first trip on 31 July 1971 with Apollo-15 astronauts David Scott and James Irwin.

Modern Explorations

Since the 1990s, Japan's Institute of Space and Aeronautical Sciences, the European Space Agency, the Chinese Lunar Exploration Agency, and the Indian Space Research Organisation have all successfully sent missions to the Moon. The first private enterprise to do so was the Manfred Memorial Moon Mission (4M), launched on 23 October 2014. On 3 January 2019, China's Chang'e 4 (named after the Moon goddess) became the first mission to achieve a soft landing directly on the far side of the Moon!

In Real Life

Neil Armstrong's words "One small step for man, one giant leap for mankind" were not the first words said on the Moon. In reality, the first words were a practical post-landing checklist! Armstrong's first communication from the Moon was simply, "Houston, Tranquillity Base here. The Eagle has landed."

▲ *The Lunar Reconnaissance Orbiter orbiting the Moon and mapping its polar regions*

Space Missions: Inner Planets

While the US was planning its many missions to the Moon, the Soviet Union was aiming for other planets. On 12 February 1961, Venera-1 became the first probe launched to another planet—Venus. Though the probe failed, the Venera series made steady progress. On 18 October 1967, a capsule from Venera-4 entered Venus's atmosphere and successfully took direct measurements. Since then, great leaps have been made in the exploration of the Inner Planets and of the asteroid belt on the group's outer boundary.

◀ *Launched by the US on 27 August 1962 on the Atlas Agena B rocket, Mariner-2 was the first space probe to fly by Venus and record the planet's temperature and atmospheric data*

Mercury

The least explored of the Inner Planets, Mercury has been visited only by the Mariner-10 and the MESSENGER. The Mariner-10 photographed about 45 per cent of Mercury over 1974–1975, while orbiting the Sun. The MESSENGER flew by Mercury three times in 2008–2009. It entered the planet's orbit in 2011, mapped it completely and continued to collect data till 30 April 2015. The latest mission to Mercury, the BepiColombo, was launched jointly by Europe and Japan in late 2018. It is expected to achieve its first flight by the planet in 2021 and stay in orbit till 2028.

▲ *This false-colour image of Mercury taken by MESSENGER shows cliff-like landforms that look like stairs. These geologically young features mean that the planet is still contracting and, like Earth, is tectonically active*

Venus

Many spacecrafts have visited Venus, most notably the Soviet Union's Venera series. In 1969, Venera 5 and 6 were the first to deploy multiple instruments and **landers** into Venus's atmosphere. On 27 March 1972, Venera-8 successfully landed on Venus's surface. Japan's Akatsuki (meaning Dawn) space probe is currently in orbit, studying the planet's atmosphere and gravity.

◀ *A radar image of Venus within the clouds, taken by NASA's Magellan on 29 October 1991*

▲ *A photo of Venus, taken by NASA's Mariner-10, shows a planet hidden under thick sulphuric clouds*

Mars

Mars has been the destination of several orbiters, landers, and rovers since the 1960s. Launched in 2001, NASA's Mars Odyssey orbiter is the longest-serving spacecraft around Mars. It will most likely remain there till 2025. The Indian Space Research Organisation (ISRO) has also placed its Mars Orbiter Mission into orbit on 24 September 2014. It is the fourth space agency to reach Mars after USSR, USA, and Europe. India is also the only country to have achieved success in its first attempt.

◀ *On 2 December 1971, Mars-3 became the first spacecraft to soft-land an instrument-bearing pod on the planet. At the time, there was a planet-wide dust storm and the pod could send back data for only 20 seconds*

Mars Rover

On 4 July 1997, the US lander called Mars Pathfinder sent out a robotic motor vehicle called Sojourner to explore the surface of Mars. This was the first Mars rover. In January 2004, the twin rovers Spirit and Opportunity also landed on Mars. They reported great discoveries such as the presence of liquid water in the past. The largest, fastest, and most advanced rover till now is NASA's Curiosity, which joined the twins on 6 August 2012.

▲ NASA's latest spacecraft, MAVEN, near Mars. The planet can be seen with its northern ice cap, Planum Boreum. Its southern polar cap is called Planum Australe

Isn't It Amazing!

Martian windstorms and dust devils actually cleaned the twin rovers' solar panels, which increased their lifespan!

The Asteroid Belt

Asteroids are airless rocks that orbit the Sun. They mainly lie in a belt just beyond Mars. The largest object in the asteroid belt is Ceres. It was discovered in 1801 by astronomer Giuseppe Piazzi. There are now 781,692 known asteroids and we are still counting. Launched on 17 February 1996, NEAR Shoemaker was the first dedicated asteroid probe. It photographed 253 Mathilde in 1997 and landed on 433 Eros in 2001. In 2010, the Japanese Hayabusa became the first probe to send back asteroid samples.

▼ The rover Opportunity in a Martian crater

21 Lutetia
253 Mathilde
243 Ida
(243) Ida I Dactyl
433 Eros
951 Gaspra
2867 Šteins
4 Vesta
25143 Itokawa

▲ A representation of the comparative sizes of eight asteroids

Space Missions: Outer Planets

The Outer Planets of our solar system lie beyond the asteroid belt. They are Jupiter, Saturn, Uranus, and Neptune. Beyond Neptune is the Kuiper Belt, a region of icy rocks and dwarf planets like Pluto. Even beyond this, forming the boundary of the solar system is the mysterious Oort Cloud, a collection of comets and unexplored matter. While Jupiter's atmosphere has been explored by a handful of spacecrafts, only four missions have been to Saturn and just one to each of the planets farther away.

▲ In 1995, NASA's Galileo became the first spacecraft to orbit Jupiter. It captured these clear images of Jupiter's four largest moons—Io, Europa, Ganymede, and Callisto

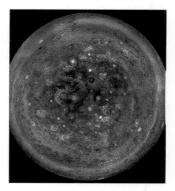

▲ Since 2016, the space probe Juno has been keeping an eye on Jupiter, sending photos such as this image of a storm on the planet's south pole in 2017

The Pioneer Programme

Beginning in 1958, the US sent a series of unmanned space missions under its Pioneer programme. The earliest of these missions were simply attempts to leave Earth. The greatest successes of the programme came with the launch of Pioneer 10 and 11 in the 1970s. Both explored the Outer Planets and left the solar system.

Pioneer-10

Launched on 2 March 1972, Pioneer-10 became the first spacecraft to go beyond the asteroid belt. It began photographing Jupiter in November 1973 and sent back some 500 images.

Its instruments gathered groundbreaking data on the planet's environment. Pioneer-10 then became the first man-made object to gather enough velocity (**escape velocity**) to leave the solar system. Its last, weak radio signal was received on 23 January 2003, when the probe was 12 billion kilometres away.

💡 Isn't It Amazing!

Just in case they meet extra-terrestrial intelligence someday, Pioneer 10 and 11 carry a plaque with information about Earth and drawings of a man and a woman.

▶ *The plaque aboard Pioneer 10 and 11*

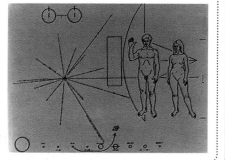

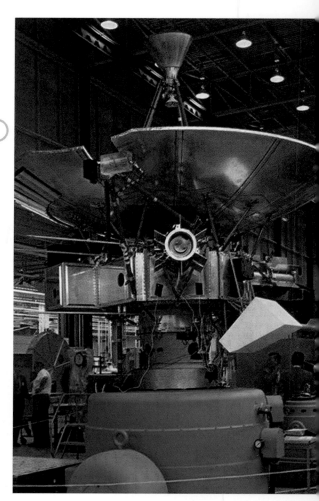

▲ *The 258 kilogram Pioneer-10 under construction*

🔍 The Voyagers

Launched in 1977, the robotic probes Voyager 1 and 2 aimed to study the outer solar system. Over these 40-plus years, they have made a string of grand discoveries such as active volcanoes on Io, a possible ocean underneath the icy crust of Europa, methane clouds and rain on Titan, Neptune's Great Dark Spot and geysers in the polar cap of Triton (Neptune's moon).

In August 2002, Voyager-1 became the first spacecraft to leave the **heliosphere** and enter **interstellar space**. Voyager-2 is the only spacecraft to have visited Uranus and Neptune. It followed Voyager-1 into interstellar space in November 2018. Both probes are still sending back information through the Deep Space Network *(see pp 16–17)*

▲ *The eruption of volcano Loki on Jupiter's moon Io was captured on film by Voyager-1*

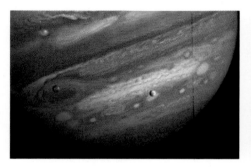

◀ *Voyager-2's photos of Neptune from 1989 show its storms—the Great Dark Spot, the bright white Scooter just below it and Dark Spot 2 (farther down) with its bright centre*

▲ *Voyager–1 took this photo of Io and Europa on 13 February 1979. Lo is about 3,50,000 kilometres above Jupiter's Great Red Spot; Europa is about 600,000 kilometres above Jupiter's clouds*

🔍 Cassini-Huygens

Launched on 15 October 1997, Cassini-Huygens is a joint mission between NASA, ESA, and the Italian Space Agency to study Saturn, its rings and its moons. The main probe, NASA's Cassini, was active for almost 20 years, photographing Venus, Earth, the asteroid 2685 Masursky, Jupiter and, of course, Saturn and its environs. Also, on board is the ESA's Huygens lander, which landed on Titan, Saturn's largest moon. The mission was a huge success and even gave scientists an idea of where else we might find life in the solar system.

▶ *In March 2012, Cassini photographed a huge storm churning through Saturn's atmosphere*

🔍 New Horizons

Launched in 2006 as part of NASA's New Frontiers programme, New Horizons explored Pluto in 2015 and is now heading towards the Kuiper belt objects.

 In Real Life

Launched on 5 April 1973, Pioneer-11 became the first craft to make direct observations of Saturn.

▶ *This image of Pluto, taken in 2015 by New Horizons, shows its icy 'heart' of nitrogen and methane*

Artificial Satellites

The idea of putting a man-made object into orbit around Earth was proposed as early as 1928. Slovenian rocket engineer Herman Potocnik (1892–1929) described how we could communicate with such a satellite using radio signals. He also described a space station and its usefulness in Earth-related experiments. Since then, human beings have developed many kinds of satellites. There are close to 2,000 satellites around our planet. Inventors have also created sophisticated networking systems to communicate with them.

► An Advanced Extremely High Frequency (AEHF) communications satellite

Deep Space Network

The awe-inspiring Deep Space Network (DSN) is an array of giant radio antennae located in three far-flung places—California, USA; near Madrid, Spain; and near Canberra, Australia. This careful placement allows DSN to remain in continuous contact with spacecrafts, even as our planet keeps rotating. The DSN guides spacecrafts and probes that are travelling far in space. It also receives information and photographs from these unmanned explorers. Furthermore, DSN communicates with some satellites orbiting Earth and studies celestial objects using radio frequencies.

▲ The Deep Space Network operations room in California, USA

Building a Satellite

These days, a satellite is designed to be strong and as light as possible. It is made of a platform (called bus) which contains the main systems. This includes batteries, computers, and engine thrusters. The antennae, solar cells, and instruments for research and communication are attached to the bus. The solar cells are usually designed on the foldable wings that are many metres long. Satellites are also covered with blankets of aluminium foil that can protect it from extreme heat and cold.

► Miniature satellites, such as this Estonian CubeSat, weigh less than 500 kilograms and serve many purposes, including data gathering and signal relay

▼ The giant parabolic antennae of the DSN are located in a bowl-shaped area created by hills to increase the antennae's sensitivity to specific radio signals

Finding the Way

The Global Positioning System (GPS) in your car, which tells you how to get from one place to another, functions because of navigation satellites. These are the same satellites that guide ships, aircrafts, and many other important systems. Navigation satellite systems that offer global coverage are called Global Navigation Satellite Systems (GNSS). The USA's GPS and Russia's GLONASS are two powerful examples of GNSS.

▶ *The highly precise and detailed maps that show you the way while you drive use time signals from navigation satellites*

Communication & Entertainment

Our TVs, phones, radios, and Internet all work on light signals or electromagnetic waves transmitted by communication satellites. Since these signals can only travel in straight lines, multiple satellites work together to transmit signals around the globe. Active satellites receive signals from a source, amplify it and redirect it to the receiver. Passive satellites simply receive and redirect a signal.

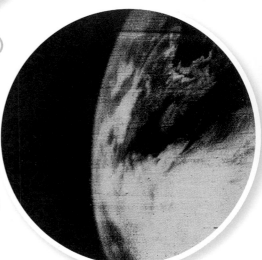

Monitoring the Weather

About 36,000 kilometres above us are geostationary satellites that track weather patterns and changes. **Geostationary** means that the satellite keeps up with Earth's spin, so it is always looking down on us from the same spot. The polar satellite is another kind of weather satellite. It orbits at right angles to the equator—about 800 kilometres above us—and passes around the North Pole and South Pole.

▲ *The first television image of Earth taken from TIROS-1, the first successful weather satellite*

Planet Observation

Earth observation satellites detect changes in our planet's green cover, ocean surfaces, and radiation. They also map Earth. Along with communications satellites, they are used by military and spy agencies to collect information that is of national importance. When used for such a purpose, they are called reconnaissance satellites.

▼ *The A-Train constellation of 2014 refers to seven Earth-observation satellites, though some of them are no longer an active part of the system*

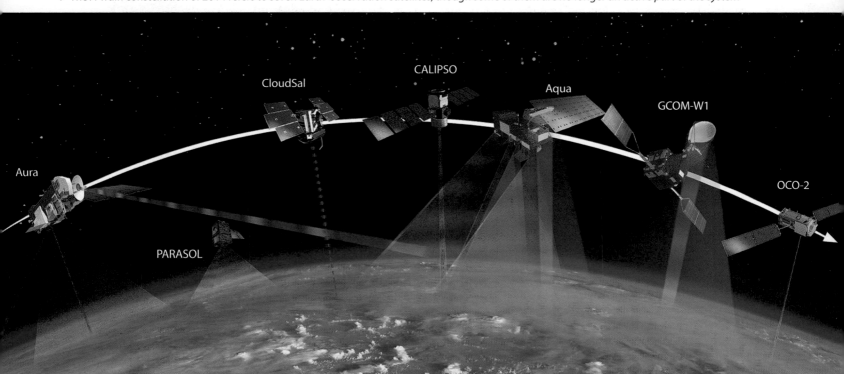

Aura

PARASOL

CloudSal

CALIPSO

Aqua

GCOM-W1

OCO-2

Galaxy, Intelsat, and Television

Galaxy is the name given to a series of over 30 communications satellites. They are owned and operated by the Intelsat Corporation. On 6 April 1965, Intelsat-1 (also known as Early Bird) became the first commercial communications satellite. Launched on 28 June 1983, Galaxy-1 was among the earliest geostationary satellites. Intelsat's network of satellites showed us worldwide events like the Olympic Games. Even the hotline that connects the White House (USA) and the Kremlin (Russia) is linked over Intelsat's satellites.

◀ The Intelsat–IVA communications satellite under construction in the 1970s

Navstar GPS

The US government's satellite-based navigation system is called Navstar GPS. Its first satellite, Block-I, was launched in 1978. Nine more followed soon. Over 1989–1994, a new series of 24 Block-II satellites were sent to complete the GPS system. Each satellite weighs about 900 kgs and has 17 m long solar panels. The key GPS part are 12 helical antennae and one spear-like antenna; they send and receive signals.

Incredible Individuals

British science fiction writer Arthur C Clarke is often called the inventor of communications satellites. In 1945, he proposed a global communications system that worked using three satellites spaced equally apart while orbiting Earth.

◀ Arthur C Clarke on the sets of the epic science fiction film , which was an adaptation of his novel, 2001: A Space Odyssey

In Real Life

The first public satellite TV signals sent from America to millions of TVs in England and France were relayed over the Telstar satellite on 23 July 1962.

Misty the Spy

Key Hole (KH) refers to a series of US reconnaissance satellites. The latest KH-13 is also known as Misty, an Enhanced Imaging System that was launched in the late 90s. It is said to be about 18,143.7 kgs in weight, but the mission is so confidential that its details cannot be confirmed. Even the satellite's name keeps changing! It is considered to be spying by taking photographs, but the subjects of these photographs remain a tightly guarded secret.

▼ Declassified in 2011, the KH-9 reconnaissance satellite—code named HEXAGON and commonly known as Big Bird—was exhibited to the public for a single day

◀ A depiction of the Block-II Navstar GPS satellite

TERRA Observes Earth

Launched on 18 December 1999, the TERRA polar orbiter is the flagship satellite of NASA's Earth Observing System. The size of a small bus, TERRA travels from North Pole to South Pole once every 99 minutes. On 6 October 2018, it completed 100,000 orbits. Terra carries five remote sensors that measure Earth's atmosphere, ocean, land, snow, ice, and energy budget. These remote sensors are ASTER, CERES, MISR, MOPITT, and MODIS.

▲ *TERRA photographed the horrific Deepwater Horizon oil spill off the Louisiana coast on 30 April 2010. When seen from space, this spill appears in the shape of two interlocking commas. It is one of the largest marine oil-slicks in human history*

▶ *GOES-13 satellite travelling to space on the Delta–IV rocket*

GOES, NOAA, and Weather Monitoring

The National Oceanic and Atmospheric Administration (NOAA) is a US agency that monitors the atmosphere and water bodies of Earth. Its geostationary GOES series of satellites focus on distinct parts of the planet, by being vigilant to the atmospheric changes that lead to storms, tornadoes, flash floods, and hurricanes. NOAA also has a series of polar satellites that spin around the globe, and keeps a close eye upon the early warning signs of climatic catastrophes.

LANDSAT: Recording Human Impact on Earth

Launched on 23 July 1972, the Earth Resources Technology satellite was eventually renamed LANDSAT. The programme since then, has sent about seven more satellites to take millions of images of the planet. The record now shows significant global changes in farmlands, forests, urban, and suburban spreads. The images are studied by map-makers and are extensively used by educators as well. LANDSAT is now the longest-running programme on Earth observation.

▶ *LANDSAT 7 was launched in 1999*

Space Agencies: Our Explorers

There are currently 72 government-run space agencies in the world. Private agencies such as SpaceX are also making progress in this conquest.

🔍 China National Space Administration (CNSA)

China's space programme began in the 1950s with the ex-NASA talent Qian Xuesen. The CNSA itself was established in 1993. In 2003, China became the third country in the world to send a man to space. In

2019, the Chang'e 4 achieved the first soft landing on the dark side of the Moon!

◀ *Yang Liwei became China's first taikonaut (Chinese astronaut) when he travelled to space on the Shenzou-5 on 15 October 2003*

🔍 European Space Agency (ESA)

An organisation of 22 countries, the ESA was established in 1975. It has paved the way for unified and peaceful developments in space.

ESA also runs Envisat, the world's largest, most complex environmental satellite.

◀ *ESA's Artemis is Europe's most advanced telecommunications satellite*

🔍 Roscosmos

Roscosmos handles the cosmonautics programmes for Russia. Some of its most interesting research involves sending up geckos, silkworm eggs, seeds, fruit flies, mushrooms and other life forms to study space biology.

🔍 Japan Aerospace Exploration Agency (JAXA)

Japan's space exploration began in the mid-1950s, led by the brilliant Hideo Itokawa. JAXA was formed on 1 October 2003. It handles technological development and advanced missions such as exploration of asteroids. JAXA is the first agency to obtain asteroid samples through a successful return mission.

▶ *Tanegashima Space Center launching JAXA's H-IIA rocket with the lunar orbit explorer Kaguya*

🔍 National Aeronautics and Space Administration (NASA)

The USA's space research and missions are handled by NASA, which explores the universe through robots and satellites. NASA furthers Earth and Sun research through its Earth Observing System and the Heliophysics Research Program.

▲ *NASA astronaut Ed White performing the first US spacewalk on Gemini-4*

🔍 Indian Space Research Organisation (ISRO)

India's space programme was founded by the scientist Vikram Sarabhai. ISRO itself was formed in 1969. Its first satellite, Aryabhata, was launched in 1975. ISRO's 2014 Mars Orbiter Mission made India the first nation to reach the planet in its first attempt! In 2017, ISRO launched a record 104 satellites on a single rocket.

Telescopes: A Distant Look

Space scientists these days have incredibly powerful telescopes locked on to far-off galaxies and planets. They even have telescopes in space. These astronomical satellites study the cosmos without suffering from any atmospheric disturbances. The idea of space telescopes came from physicist Lyman Spitzer in 1946. The first successful one, the OAO-2, was launched by the US in 1968.

▼ The Hubble Space Telescope

Space Telescopes

NASA's 'Great Observatories' refers to four powerful space telescopes. The Compton Gamma Ray Observatory observes **gamma rays** in space, the Chandra Observatory observes **X-rays**, the Spitzer Space Telescope observes **infrared rays**, and the Hubble Space Telescope observes visible light.

◄ Images from Chandra, Hubble, and Spitzer combined show the Crab Nebula spewing energy at the rate of 100,000 Suns

Gemini Observatory

Famous for its twin 8.1 m diameter telescopes, the Gemini Observatory is located in the mountains of Hawaii and Chile. From here, Gemini's telescopes are able to keep the entire sky under scrutiny.

European Southern Observatory (ESO)

Created in 1962, ESO observes the skies from three sites in the Atacama Desert, Chile—La Silla, Paranal, and Chajnantor. With its 3.6 m New Technology Telescope, ESO invented the method of using computers to control telescopes' mirrors. ESO also runs the Very Large Telescope (VLT), which discovered the first **exoplanet**. The VLT is currently observing stars that are close to the supermassive black hole at the centre of our galaxy.

WM Keck Observatory

The two-telescope WM Keck Observatory lies 4,145 m high, near the peak of old volcano Mauna Kea, in Hawaii. With their 10 m primary mirrors, these telescopes are among the largest astronomical telescopes in the world. They are responsible for achievements such as discovering the existence of galaxies at the edge of the universe and studying supernovas to find out how fast the universe is expanding.

▶ Located at the Roque de los Muchachos Observatory in the Canaries, Spain, the 10.4 m Gran Telescopio Canarias is the largest single-aperture optical telescope in the world

Isn't It Amazing!

The ESO 3.6 m telescope uses an instrument called HARPS, which has discovered 130 extrasolar planets till date!

▲ Located 2,400 m high in the mountains of the Atacama Desert, La Silla has several sophisticated optical telescopes pointed towards the sky

Bright-tailed Comets

Comets are small bodies of frozen gas, rock, and dust orbiting the Sun. They are leftover material from the formation of our solar system about 4.6 billion years ago. When a comet comes closer to the Sun, its dust and gas starts to heat up and escape. This gives the comet a glowing head and a tail that can stretch for millions of miles!

The comet is made of the nucleus (the solid, stable part), the coma (a dense cloud of water and gases), the dust tail (made of millions of kilometres of smoke-sized particles) and the ion tail (composed of several hundred million kilometres of plasma and ions)

◄ *The long-period comet Hale-Bopp was so bright and large, it was called the Great Comet of 1997. It was discovered on 23 July 1995, independently by both Alan Hale and Thomas Bopp*

⭐ Incredible Individuals

Comets were discovered in ancient times. Most notably, Halley's Comet first appeared in Chinese records of c. 240 BCE. It appeared again in the beautiful Bayeux Tapestry that depicts the conquest of England in 1066.

▲ *The star of Bethlehem in Giotto's mesmerising Adoration of the Magi (c.1305) is said to be inspired by Halley's Comet, spotted four years before the date of this painting*

🔍 Where do Comets come From?

In 1951, astronomer Gerard Kuiper correctly proposed that comets come from a belt of icy bodies beyond Neptune. The force of the Sun's gravity draws some of these objects inwards into a closer orbit. These are called short-period comets. They take less than 200 years to complete a single orbit of the Sun. Long-period comets arrive from a region even beyond the Kuiper belt. This mysterious region at the edge of our solar system is called the Oort Cloud. The comets here can take up to 30 million years to complete their orbit!

Halley's Comet

The short-period Halley's Comet can be seen by the naked eye as it comes close to the Sun. This last occurred in 1986 and will happen again in 2061. It is named after English astronomer Edmond Halley, who first predicted the comet's periodic occurrence. During the 1986 appearance, several probes were launched to study the comet more closely. Photos from the Soviet Vega-1 started surfacing on 4 March 1986. These included the first-ever image of its nucleus. Others that successfully studied the comet are Vega 2, the ESA's Giotto, and the two Japanese probes Suisei and Sakigake. Together, they are all known as the Halley Armada.

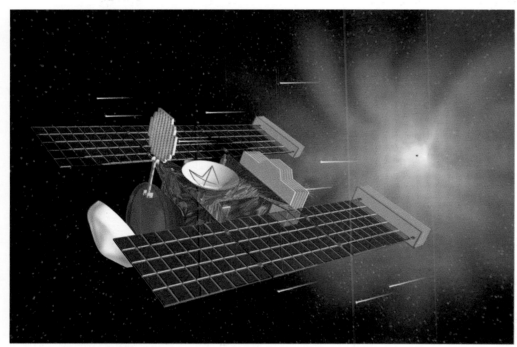

▲ *Launched on 7 February 1999, the 390 kg Stardust space probe visited comet Wild-2 and brought back the first samples of comet dust on 15 January 2006*

◄ *On 4 July 2005, NASA's Deep Impact space probe successfully sent an impactor to collide with the comet Tempel-1 (resulting in a bright flare) to study questions on impact craters and comet composition*

Rosetta Probe

The ESA's Rosetta space probe was launched on 2 March 2004 to study the comet 67P/Churyumov–Gerasimenko. It reached the comet on 6 August 2014 and settled into the orbit within 10–30 kms of the body. On 12 November, Rosetta sent out its lander module Philae, which made the first successful landing on a comet. The probe was thus able to make detailed studies, rendering the mission a triumph for the agency.

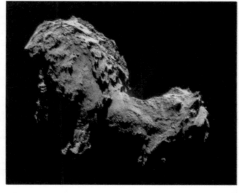

▲ *Rosetta's photo of comet Churyumov–Gerasimenko*

Jean-Louis Pons (1761–1831), a self-taught French astronomer, discovered a record 37 comets over 1801–1827. The other prolific discoverer of comets was British-born American William Robert Brooks (1844–1921).

Caroline Herschel (1750–1848), a lauded German astronomer, was the first woman to discover a series of comets.

Gottfried Kirch (1639–1710) made the first telescopic discovery of a comet—the Komet C/1680 V1, also called Kirch's Comet.

Edward Emerson Barnard (1857–1923) was the first to discover a comet through photographic methods. This was comet 206P/Barnard-Boattini, on the night of 13 October 1892.

Incidents and Accidents

Human exploration of space has been an odyssey of hair-raising exploits and tragic misadventures. We owe a great deal to our heroic space pioneers. Each small step of their cosmic tussle has led to giant leaps in our understanding of the universe.

23 March 1961

The first space-related fatality occur red during a low-pressure endurance experiment. A Soviet fighter pilot and trainee cosmonaut dropped an alcohol-soaked cloth on a hotplate. Extra oxygen in the chamber (50 per cent, compared to the 21 per cent in normal air) led to a fire, and killed Valentin Bondarenko.

17 May 1930

Austrian rocketry pioneer Max Valier died in a rocket-engine explosion in Berlin, becoming the first tragic casualty of the modern space age.

▲ *Valier in a rocket car*

18 March 1965

Alexei Leonov's famous first spacewalk nearly ends in disaster when his spacesuit inflates while he was still in the vacuum of space. It became so big that he was unable to re-enter the spacecraft. Fortunately, he was able to open a valve and let off some of the pressure from the suit.

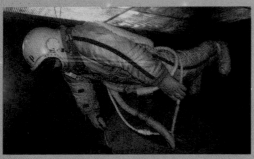
▲ *Leonov's spacesuit*

Leonov's spacesuit deflated just enough for him to re-enter the capsule. The spacecraft became so cramped, the crew's landing got affected. They ended up in a deep forest and spent a frigid couple of nights in makeshift huts, before a helicopter flied to their rescue.

24 April 1967

The first in-flight tragedy in the history of the space age affected Soyuz-1. Its sole crewman, Colonel Vladimir Komarov died after the craft's parachutes failed to open during descent and the capsule crashed into the ground.

⊛ Incredible Individuals

During the Apollo 14 mission of 1971, the American astronaut Alan Shepard became the first and only person to hit golf balls on the Moon. The balls are still up there!

▲ *Alexei Leonov*

14 November 1969

Apollo 12 became the sixth manned mission to the Moon. During its launch, it was struck by lightning twice! The crew spent extra time in orbit ensuring that there was no damage that would affect their mission to the Moon.

▲ The 'Fallen Astronaut' is a small sculpture on the Moon which, along with a commemorative plaque, honours pioneering cosmonauts such as Komarov

7 February 1984

Astronauts often tether themselves to a spacecraft while walking out in space. Bruce McCandless achieved the first untethered spacewalk on Challenger mission STS-41-B.

◄ McCandless on his famous untethered spacewalk

25 July 1984

During the Soyuz T-12 mission, Svetlana Savitskaya became the first woman to take a spacewalk.

28 January 1986

The Space Shuttle Challenger disintegrated 73 seconds into its lift-off. Cold weather caused one of its seals to fail, which in turn let in hot gases from the rocket and led to the disaster. The tragedy claimed the lives of all seven crew members.

▲ The Challenger explosion

17 June 1985

Royal Saudi Air Force pilot Sultan bin Salman bin Abdulaziz Al Saud became the first member of royalty to fly to outer space. He still holds the record for being the youngest person to fly on the Space Shuttle, at the age of 28.

◄ Al Saud on his NASA mission

11 March 2001

Susan J Helms and James S Voss set the record for the longest time spent outside a space vehicle at 8 hours and 56 minutes.

▲ Helms viewing Earth from a window on the ISS

1 February 2003

Space Shuttle Columbia's left wing failed while re-entering the atmosphere after a two-week mission. The entire capsule broke apart 65 kms above Earth and fell in fragments over Texas and Louisiana, USA. All seven crew members lost their lives.

► Remembering the crew of Columbia: (from left) mission specialist David Brown, commander Rick Husband, mission specialist Laurel Clark, mission specialist Kalpana Chawla, mission specialist Michael Anderson, pilot William McCool, and Israeli payload specialist Ilan Ramon

Space Stations: Stellar Base Camps

▲ *A 1971 stamp commemorating Salyut-1 and its three brave astronauts*

Certain artificial satellites stay in low Earth orbit and people can live inside them. These are called space stations. The earliest such station was Salyut-1, launched by the Soviet Union on 19 April 1971. It was built as one complete piece and sent up to space; the crew followed afterwards. Space stations have come a long way since then.

▲ *The International Space Station with its vast array of solar panels*

🔍 The Salyut Programme

Over 1971–1986, the Soviet Union explored the possibility of living in space. They called the mission Salyut. Over these 15 years, they successfully sent up four space stations for scientific research and two for military purposes. All six had human crew members. Of course, there were failures too. Two other Salyut launches failed. The world's first manned mission to a space station, Salyut-1, ended in grief when the crew died just before re-entry to Earth. On 30 June 1971, a pressure valve on the descending Soyuz-11 opened too early, suffocating the three astronauts.

💡 Isn't It Amazing!

During its launch, Skylab hit a micro-meteoroid. The impact deprived the craft of electricity and thermal protection! Fortunately, the crew was able to repair Skylab. It was the first time such a large repair was conducted in space.

▶ *Astronauts building part of a space station as it orbits Earth*

Skylab

Skylab, NASA's first space station, was inhabited for some 24 weeks over 1973–1974. It bore a solar observatory (Apollo Telescope Mount), two docking ports, EVA capabilities, and a main working area called Orbital Workshop. Skylab teams made breakthrough progress in solar science and Earth observation. They also broke Salyut's record of longest stay in space, taking it from 23 days to 84 days.

 ## Mir

The first space station to be put together in space was the Soviet Union's Mir. The core unit and modules (with specific functions) were launched separately and assembled in orbit over 1986–1996. This became the standard way of building space stations. Mir was continuously inhabited for 3,644 days. It still holds the record for the longest single human space flight. Over 1994–1995, astronaut Valeriy Polyakov spent 437 days and 18 hours on the space station.

▶ A view of the Mir Space Station from Endeavour

 ## The International Space Station (ISS)

The ISS is the biggest man-made object that has ever flown in space. It orbits Earth 16 times a day. Five space agencies came together to create the ISS—NASA, Roscosmos, JAXA, ESA, and CSA (Canada). Its first component, Zarya was launched in 1998. Its first permanent crew arrived on Expedition-1 on 2 November 2000. ISS has since been occupied continuously for over 19 years! The space station has been visited by cosmonauts and even tourists from 18 nations.

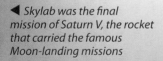

◀ Skylab was the final mission of Saturn V, the rocket that carried the famous Moon-landing missions

▶ Astronauts floating in zero gravity inside the ISS

Living in Space

As you can imagine, living in outer space is vastly different from living on Earth. The atmosphere, gravity, warmth, water, regular day-and-night cycles, and even the freedom to move about are simply not possible in space. Large teams of people have been working to recreate the well-being of life on Earth for astronauts in space vehicles and stations.

◄ *Astronauts on the ISS rise from their sleeping quarters on Christmas morning in 2010*

🔍 Mental Fitness

Cosmonauts on the early space stations like Salyut and Mir were the first to show signs of mental stress from extended stays in outer space. Their experience led the Russians to set up studies in aerospace psychology. In the mid-1990s, Russian space psychologists shared their insights with NASA. Today's aerospace psychologists ensure that the people going up to space possess strong, sturdy minds. They also support the astronauts throughout training, the mission and in adjusting to life after the mission.

▲ *Mealtime aboard the ISS*

🔍 Zero Gravity

In space, a body has no weight. Astronauts simply float from one place to another. Without any work to do, their back and legs quickly lose muscle density. Even the heart, which is a muscle, shrinks in size. Without the need for a strong skeleton, bones lose calcium, which forms stones in the kidneys. Blood and body fluids settle in the upper body (instead of flowing downwards). This makes astronauts puffy and congested, as if they have a bad cold. Since the absence of gravity means that there is no 'up' or 'down' in space, most astronauts get space-sick. They suffer from nausea, headaches, and even find it hard to locate their own limbs! To minimise these issues, astronauts exercise regularly while in space.

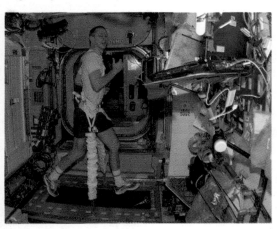

▶ *Astronaut Marsha Ivins in zero-gravity outer space*

◄ *ESA astronaut Frank De Winne exercising on a special treadmill in the ISS*

From Food to Waste

Early astronauts took their food in the form of food cubes, dehydrated meals or mush in aluminium tubes. Nowadays, they have a choice of 150 different types of food. Brushing teeth is very similar to what you do on Earth. Except, there are no sinks that let out water, so astronauts spit into a washcloth. They also use washcloths with special soaps and shampoos to clean their bodies without water. It is impossible to do laundry in space, so they take along several sets of underwear! On the Space Shuttle, there are four trash bins with trash liners that are sealed as soon as they are full.

▲ Food for astronauts comes in various forms

▲ The toilet on board the Zvezda space module

► Astronaut Cady Coleman washing her hair with special shampoo on the space station

Incredible Individuals

Cosmonaut Anatoly Solovyev holds the record for the most spacewalks. He undertook 16 of them.

▲ Astronaut Anatoly Solovyev suiting up for a space walk

Spacesuits

When astronauts leave a spacecraft, they do so wearing a protective spacesuit. It is made of interchangeable parts that can be adjusted to fit various sizes. The suit is made of modern materials like Ortho-Fabric and aluminised Mylar, to which metal parts are attached. It is puncture-proof and equipped with cameras, drinking-water and even a diaper-like pouch to contain urine. Inventors began building full-pressure suits for extreme altitudes in the 1930s. The first one to be worn in outer space was the Soviet SK-1 suit, worn by Yuri Gagarin.

The Future of Space Exploration

With so many agencies focused on space exploration, the frontiers of human existence are being steadily pushed outwards. Private enterprises such as SpaceX and Mars One are even concentrating on colonising Mars. With space probes discovering water, atmosphere, and other conditions conducive to life out there, human presence on alien planets may soon be a reality.

Star Wars

Spy satellites and anti-satellite weapons are already a modern-day reality. In the 1950s, the US even considered bombing the Moon to display their technological might. Since then, many countries have developed their own nuclear weapons and missile capabilities. In the late 60s, the US, UK, and Soviet Union entered into an Outer Space Treaty. This laid out principles for exploration and use of outer space and celestial bodies. For instance, it specifies that no weapons testing, or military actions can be carried out on the Moon or on any celestial body. As of February 2019, over 100 countries have signed this treaty, which forms the basis for international space law. While the treaty bans weapons of mass destruction, it sadly does not prevent the use of conventional weapons in space.

Space Tourism

As reusable rockets and cheaper rocket technology come into existence, large-scale space tourism could really take off in the near future. The Russian space agency has already taken tourists to Earth's orbit. In 2001, American multimillionaire Dennis Tito paid to visit outer space and became the first space tourist. He spent close to eight days in orbit. In 1985, Christa McAuliffe, a school teacher, was chosen to fly to space; tragically, she was on board the disastrous Challenger mission. In 2006, the Iranian-American engineer Anousheh Ansari became the first female space tourist.

▶ *In the 1990s, eight people were asked to live in the isolated Biosphere-2 habitat for two long years, so scientists could understand the needs of human beings who might colonise a new world*

▶ *Ever since Chandrayaan-1 discovered lunar water, there is renewed interest in establishing a colony on the Moon*

Colonising Space

Many people believe that it is necessary to colonise other planets, in case Earth is destroyed by natural disasters—or through human greed and recklessness! Many enterprises have been set up with this goal in mind. No human beings have landed on another planet yet. So, we are still a long way from creating the controlled living environment needed for colonisation and survival. As interplanetary robotic probes send back more information from the solar system, our scientists are steadily developing the large-scale technologies that will be needed to power human life in an alien world.

▲ Anousheh Ansari with a grass plant on board the ISS

Incredible Individuals

The billionaire and founder of Cirque du Soleil, Guy Laliberte is also an accordion player, a fire-eater, and a stilt-walker. In 2009, he became Canada's first space tourist on a mission to raise awareness about water issues on our planet. This was the first social mission to space.

▲ Guy Laliberte (centre) along with American and Russian astronauts waving farewell before taking off on their flight to the ISS

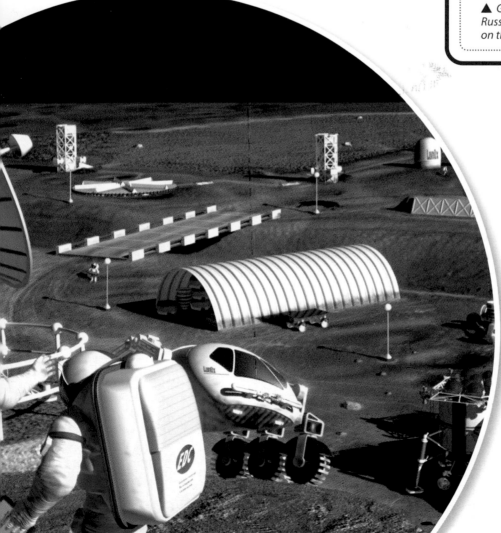

▶ A US Air Force F-15 Eagle launching an anti-satellite missile

Word Check

Ancient Civilizations

Alloys: In the making of metals, alloys are formed by mixing two or more pure metals. This creates new types of metals that are suitable for different technologies.

Assyria: It is a historical region and civilisation, not to be confused with Syria! At its peak, Assyria stretched from northern Mesopotamia through modern Turkey and down to Egypt.

Bipedal: Using two legs for walking.

c.: This is an abbreviation for the word 'circa', which means about or approximately.

Cro-Magnon: It is an erect and tall race of ancient humans of France. They were among the earliest *Homo sapiens* on Earth.

Elamite: The people of Elam, an ancient kingdom. It lay next to Sumer and stretched north from the coast of the Persian Gulf.

Fossils: The remains of a prehistoric plant or animal buried under a rock is known as a fossil. Fossils are studied to discover more about the time period to which they belong.

Hoplite: It refers to an armed foot-soldier from ancient Greece.

Leavening: It is a substance that, when mixed into a dough and baked, gives you light, fluffy foods, such as bread and cake. Modern-day leavening agents include yeast and baking powder.

Macedon: It was an ancient country in northern Greece. It was home to Alexander the Great.

Mesopotamia: It is a Greek word for 'two rivers'. This name refers to the historical area between the rivers Tigris and Euphrates. It was dominated by the Sumerian, Akkadian, Assyrian, and Babylonian civilisations.

Proto humans: They are also called archaic humans. This phrase describes closely-related human species that lived on earth thousands of years ago. This includes *Homo neanderthalensis* (Neanderthals) and *Australopithecus afarensis.* All of them are now extinct, except for *Homo sapiens*, the modern humans.

Reservoir: A man-made lake. It usually stores flood or rainwater for use during the dry season.

Scribes: Few people in ancient times knew how to read and write. Official writing and record-keeping jobs were therefore given to scholarly people called scribes.

Tutankhamun: He is possibly the most famous Pharaoh since 1922, when British archaeologist Howard Carter unearthed his treasure-filled tomb in Egypt's Valley of the Kings.

Earth Discoveries

Admiral: The chief commander of a navy.

Bay: It is a small body of water surrounded by land on three sides.

Blubber: It is the fat of mammals of the sea, such as whales and seals.

Burro: It is a small donkey.

Cartography: It is the art and science of map-making.

Conquistador: It is a title used to describe a leader in the Spanish conquest of the Americas.

Corps: It is a military unit.

Envoy or ambassador: A person who represents his or her government in a foreign nation.

Estuary: It refers to the widening arms of a river, where they meet the sea.

Expedition: It is a journey with a specific goal, usually undertaken with a group of people.

Extinct: It means that an animal or plant is no longer in existence.

Gulf: It is a part of the sea that is surrounded by land on three sides. It is larger than a bay.

Indigenous: It refers to a group of people who are native to an area.

Isthmus: It is a narrow strip of land surrounded by water on two sides.

Kinsay: It is a city that was captured by the Mongols in 1279. It helped them control all of China. With more than a million people, it was the world's largest city at the time—many times larger than the cities of Europe.

Lacquerware: These are decorative wooden objects painted with a glossy varnish called lacquer.

Marooned: It means to abandon a person on a deserted island.

Mutiny: It is a revolt against a superior officer.

Pilgrimage: It is a journey to a sacred place.

Sampans: They are narrow wooden boats used in East Asia.

Strait: It is a narrow strip of water surrounded by land on two sides.

Electronics & Communications

AM: This stands for Amplitude Modulation, a method in which sound is coded on to radio waves for transmission.

Anode: It is the positively charged electrode by which the electrons leave an electrical device.

Artificial Intelligence: The science of building machines that can imitate human thinking, interactions, and responses.

Byte: It is a unit of computer information.

It is made of 8 bits of data. Other units are given below.

Bit (b) = 0 or 1 unit
1 Byte (B) = 8 bits
1 Kilobyte (KB) = 1,024 bytes
1 Megabyte (MB) = 1,024 kilobytes
1 Gigabyte (GB) = 1,024 megabytes
1 Terabyte (TB) = 1,024 gigabytes

Cathode: It is the negatively charged electrode by which electrons enter an electrical device.

Cloud: It is a network of computers and storage devices on the Internet that allows people to store information online.

Electrical conductor: This is any material that allows electricity to flow through it. Most metals fall in this category, while materials like wood, glass, and rubber are poor conductors of electricity.

Electromagnetic: It refers to the magnetic field produced by an electric current.

Electron: It is an elementary particle that is negatively charged. The two other elementary particles are protons, which carry a positive charge, and neutrons, which carry no charge at all. Together these three elementary particles form an atom.

FM: Frequency Modulation is a way of imposing sound on to radio waves so they can be transmitted over the radio.

HTML: It is the abbreviation for hypertext markup language: a language that marks up documents for the World Wide Web. It can be used for text, art, sound, video, and hyperlinks.

Laser: It is short for Light Amplification by Stimulated Emission of Radiation. Laser is a kind of strong, focussed beam of light.

Matrix: It refers to a close-knit arrangement of elements—like a tight grid or lattice.

Microchip: It is a tiny silicon chip that can be found in many computers. It has electronic circuits that enable the chip to hold information.

Network: It refers to a group of things that are connected to each other in some way.

Photons: These are particles of light, and a type of electromagnetic radiation.

Radio waves: When electricity and magnetism interact, they produce a variety of wave-like effects called electromagnetic radiation. Many of these waves—radio waves, X-rays, microwaves, infrared rays, ultraviolet rays, gamma rays—are invisible to our eyes. Visible light, that is, all the colours of the rainbow, also consists of electromagnetic waves.

Router: It is a device that allows you to use Wi-Fi by delivering Internet data in a LAN.

Semiconductor: It is a solid substance that is used in electrical devices, as it allows electrical energy and heat to move through it.

Transistor: It is a device that uses semiconductors to control the flow of electricity in a machine.

Vacuum: It is an empty space that is free of all matter, even air. It is not possible to have a true and complete vacuum, but you can get very close to it.

Vacuum tube: Also called a valve, this electronic device looks like a light bulb, but works like a switch. When the tube is heated up, it allows electricity to flow through. When the tube is cold, the current stops.

Inventions in Motion

Accelerator: In a car, the accelerator is a pedal at the feet of the driver. Pressing it makes the car go faster.

Aerodynamics: It is the study of motion in air, and of the forces acting upon flying bodies.

Aviator: It is the operator or pilot of an aircraft.

Carburettor: It is the part of the engine where fuel and air combine and burn. The carburettor also controls the flow of air into the engine and the engine's speed.

Clutch: It is the part that connects the engine to the wheels.

Combustion: It is the process by which something is burned up.

Electromagnet: It is a magnet where the magnetic force exerted, or the magnetic field produced, is powered by electric current.

Gear shift: In vehicles, gears are used to manage speed and direction with maximum efficiency. A gear shift is the mechanism by which a driver can change gears to change speed or direction.

Locomotive: It is a big vehicle used for pulling trains.

Mach: It is a relative measurement of high speed, usually compared with the speed of sound.

NASA: The abbreviation for National Aeronautics and Space Administration, an agency that handles the USA's space research and programmes.

Pneumatic: In mechanics, this refers to an object that can be filled with air, or a system that works using air pressure.

Quadricycle: It is a cycle with four wheels.

Spark plug: It is a battery-operated gadget that sparks when a current runs through it. This provides the combustion for the engine.

Velocipede: It is a vehicle that runs on land with the force or effort exerted by human beings. The modern bicycle is a common example of a velocipede.

Victorian: It refers to an event, person, or invention from the Victorian Era or the period during which Queen Victoria ruled over the United Kingdom.

Turbine: It is a rotating engine made

using a series of curved metal plates. It moves when hit by the pressure of steam air, or water.

Water radiator: It is a cooling system that keeps the engine from overheating.

Zeppelin: It is an airship that is powered by a gigantic, bullet-shaped chamber of gas. It is named after Count Ferdinand von Zeppelin who first developed this type of airship.

Medical Inventions

Anaesthetic: It is a drug that numbs a part of your body (local anaesthetic) or puts your whole body to sleep (general anaesthetic).

Analgesic: It is a painkiller.

Anatomy: It is the study of the internal structure of living things.

Antibiotics: They are used to kill dangerous bacteria.

Appendectomy: It is the surgical removal of the appendix, a small pouch-like organ in the lower right side of your abdomen.

Bilirubin: It is a yellowish substance formed in the liver. It gives its colour to human excrement.

Biopsy: It is a test where tissue is removed from a living person to check for the cause or presence of disease.

Dermatoscope: It is a device used to examine the lesions on a patient's skin.

Dissect: It is a process by which a person methodically cuts open a dead creature (plant, animal, or human) to study its insides.

ECG: It is the abbreviation for electrocardiogram. It is a test that records your heartbeat to see if it is functioning well.

EEG: It is the abbreviation for electroencephalogram. It is a test for examining abnormalities in your brain.

Electromagnetic rays: A number of visible and invisible rays that include

X-rays, all the colours of light, microwaves, infrared rays, gamma rays, and many others.

Epidemic: It refers to the spreading of an infectious disease to a large number of people.

Germ theory: It is a medical theory stating that some diseases are caused by the presence of microorganisms (organisms that can only be seen through a microscope).

Obstetrics: It is the field of medicine that is concerned with childbirth.

Ophthalmoscope: It is the medical device used to look into a patient's eye.

Otoscope: It is the medical device that doctors use to look into a patient's ears.

Photomicrography: It refers to photographing a substance while it is kept under a microscope.

Physiology: It is the way a living being and its body parts function.

Porphyria: It is a disease affecting the blood and nervous system.

Retina: The part of your eye that receives information from light rays and transmits it to the brain.

Sphygmomanometer: A device that measures blood pressure.

Stem cell: An undifferentiated cell that can turn into a specialised cell at a later point.

Variolation: It is an obsolete technique of immunising a patient.

Space Discoveries

Aperture: In telescopes and cameras, aperture refers to the hole through which light travels to reach the instrument and our eyes (or camera film).

Astronomers: They are people who make systematic observations and records of celestial objects.

Astrophysics: It is the study of the stars and all other celestial bodies. It also combines theories and laws with observations of the universe.

Cosmology: It is the study of the universe, its formation, evolution, and future.

Escape velocity: It is the minimum speed needed to break free from the gravitational pull of a massive body. For instance, a rocket needs to travel at an escape velocity of about 11.186 kmps to get away from Earth.

Exoplanet: Also known as extrasolar planets, they are planets that orbit a star other than the Sun.

Gamma rays, X-rays, and infrared rays: They are different types of electromagnetic rays; they are like light rays, but are invisible to our eyes.

Geostationary: It refers to the orbit of a satellite that keeps up with the spin of Earth; thus, it remains above the same spot in comparison to our planet.

Heliocentrism: It is the model of the universe where the Sun is at the centre of the solar system and the other planets revolve around it.

Heliosphere: It is a massive bubble-like region around the Sun formed by solar wind.

Impactor: It is a craft that is sent out specifically to collide with a celestial object.

Interstellar space: It is the space within a galaxy that is beyond the influence of its individual stars.

Ions: They are atoms with extra electrons or missing electrons.

Lander: It is a space module that lands on celestial bodies such as asteroids, comets, planets, and natural satellites.

Plasma: It is the fourth state of matter (after solid, liquid, and gas); it is an ionized gas.

Precession: It describes the motion of a body spinning in such a way that it wobbles, so that the axis of rotation sweeps out a cone.

a: above, b: below/ bottom, c: centre, f: far, l: left, r: right, t: top, bg: background

Cover

Shutterstock: Front: Ioan Panaite; DenisNata; Nieuwland Photography; BCFC; mstanley, sumire8; Mega Pixel; Comet Design; Victor Jiang; David Herraez Calzada; Pagina
Back: sportpoint; siraphat; Artsplav; Audrius Merfeldas;

Wikimedia Commons: Front : File:1886 Starley 'Rover' Safety Cycle British Motor Museum 09-2016 (29928044262).jpg /https://commons.wikimedia.org/wiki/File:1886_Starley_%27Rover%27_Safety_Cycle_British_Motor_Museum_09-2016_(29928044262).jpg; File:Luna 1 - 2 Spacecraft.png / https://commons.wikimedia.org/wiki/File:Luna_1_-_2_Spacecraft.png; File:Tablet V of the Epic of Gilgamesh.jpg / https://commons.wikimedia.org/wiki/File:Tablet_V_of_the_Epic_of_Gilgamesh.jpg; South-pointing_chariot_(Science_Museum_model)/Andy Dingley / CC BY (https://creativecommons.org/licenses/by/3.0)/wikimedia commons; File:Drop spindle from Egypt.jpg / https://commons.wikimedia.org/wiki/File:Drop_spindle_from_Egypt.jpg; File:Concorde on Bristol.jpg / https://commons.wikimedia.org/wiki/File:Concorde_on_Bristol.jpg; File:Tut bumerangs.JPG / https://commons.wikimedia.org/wiki/File:Tut_bumerangs.JPG; Side b of body of herakles neck amphora.jpg / https://commons.wikimedia.org/wiki/File:Side_b_of_body_of_herakles_neck_amphora.jpg; File:RIAN archive 186141 Nuclear icebreaker Arktika.jpg / https://commons.wikimedia.org/wiki/File:RIAN_archive_186141_Nuclear_icebreaker_Arktika.jpg; File:Machupicchu intihuatana.JPG / https://commons.wikimedia.org/wiki/File:Machupicchu_intihuatana.JPG; File:Shuttle profiles.jpg / https://commons.wikimedia.org/wiki/File:Shuttle_profiles.jpg
Back : File:Daimler-Maybach grandfather clock engine and early carriafges at Mercedes Museum.jpg / https://commons.wikimedia.org/wiki/File:Daimler-Maybach_grandfather_clock_engine_and_early_carriafges_at_Mercedes_Museum.jpg; File:Baking mold Mari Louvre AO18902.jpg / https://commons.wikimedia.org/wiki/File:Baking_mold_Mari_Louvre_AO18902.jpg

Ancient Civilisations

Shutterstock: 3b/Procy; 3cr/Uncle Leo; 4tc/Juan Aunion; 4&5b/Nataliya Stolyar; 5tc/Mark Sheridan-Johnson; 5tr/Abeselom Zerit; 6cr/Zelenskaya; 6&7b/Homo Cosmicos; 8&9bg/Tartila; 9br/Cindy Xiong; 10tr/Yuri Turkov; 11b/Nor Gal; 14tr/cge2010; 14br/milosk50; 15tr/CRS PHOTO; 15b/mgallar; 16tl/givaga; 16tr/dagherrotipo; 16bl/zawisak; 16br/C.J. Everhardt; 17tc/Victor Jiang; 17tr/cigdem; 17bl/PaPicasso; 17br/mountainpix; 18br/Olinchuk; 19cl/subin pumsom; 19cr/Cem OZER; 20bg/HorenkO; 20tl/Kamira; 20cr/Algol; 22tl/Matt Howard; 23tl/Daniel Eskridge; 23b/m.o.arvas; 24cr/matrioshka; 24bc/Kokhanchikov; 25tr/Anatoli Styf; 25br/ChameleonsEye; 26tr/Milagli; 27cr/mountainpix; 27cr/mountainpix; 28cl/Khaled ElAdawy; 28&29bg/Seita; 29cr/Marko5; 30cr/zarzamora; 31cl/Lotus Images FX; 24&25bc/Vadim Sadovski; 26&27tc/Diego Barucco; 28background/Stefano Garau; 29tl/Tragoolchitr Jittasaiyapan; 29tc/Tragoolchitr Jittasaiyapan

Wikimedia Commons: 4br/File:Australopithecus afarensis models University of Pisa's Natural History Museum.jpg/Federigo Federighi / CC BY-SA (https://creativecommons.org/licenses/by-sa/4.0)/wikimedia commons; 5bl/File:Venus of Dolni Vestonice 2014-09-30.jpg/Miroslav Zachoval / CC BY (https://creativecommons.org/licenses/by/2.0)/wikimedia commons; 5bc/File:Ur-Nassiriyah.jpg/M.Lubinski from Iraq,USA. / CC BY-SA (https://creativecommons.org/licenses/by-sa/2.0)/wikimedia commons; 6tl/File:Bell Beaker, Copper Age, City of Prague Museum, 175585.jpg/Zde / CC BY-SA (https://creativecommons.org/licenses/by-sa/4.0)/wikimedia commons; 6br/File:DO-2346-Vognserup Enge.jpg/Lennart Larsen (CC BY-SA 2.0) / CC BY-SA (https://creativecommons.org/licenses/by-sa/2.0)/wikimedia commons; 7tl/File:Gold bracelet bull head Transylvania.jpg/Yelkrokoyade / CC BY-SA (https://creativecommons.org/licenses/by-sa/3.0)/wikimedia commons; 7tr/File:Ninevehreliefashurbanipalagainsthamanu.jpg/Ealdgyth / CC BY-SA (https://creativecommons.org/licenses/by-sa/3.0)/wikimedia commons; 7cr/File:Bronze age weapons Romania.jpg/Work of Romanian goverment / Public domain/wikimedia commons; 7cl/Alaca Hüyük dagger.jpg/Stipich Béla / CC BY-SA (http://creativecommons.org/licenses/by-sa/3.0/)/wikimedia commons; 8tl/File:Edfu6 c.jpg/Edfu6.JPG: Rémihderivative work: JMCC1 / CC BY-SA (https://creativecommons.org/licenses/by-sa/2.5)/wikimedia commons; 8tc/File:Solvognen-00100.tif/Nationalmuseet / CC BY-SA (https://creativecommons.org/licenses/by-sa/3.0)/wikimedia commons; 8&9 bc/File:1600 Himmelsscheibe von Nebra sky disk anagoria.jpg/Anagoria / CC BY (https://creativecommons.org/licenses/by/3.0)/wikimedia commons; 8bl/File:Attic Black-Figure Amphora (HARGM3804) showing A side decoration.JPG/Staff or representatives of Harrogate Museums and Arts Service / CC BY-SA (https://creativecommons.org/licenses/by-sa/4.0)/wikimedia commons; 9tl/File:BMC 06.jpg/Classical Numismatic Group, Inc. http://www.cngcoins.com / CC BY-SA (http://creativecommons.org/licenses/by-sa/3.0/)/wikimedia commons; 9tc/File:Ironie pile Bagdad.jpg/Ironie / CC BY-SA (https://creativecommons.org/licenses/by-sa/2.5)/wikimedia commons; 9tr/File:Cai-lun.jpg/Unknown author / Public domain/wikimedia commons; 10cr/File:Parigi griffe.jpg/Giulio Parigi / Public domain/wikimedia commons; 10b1/Five Steps of Papermaking - Step 1 - Cutting and Moisturizing of the Bamboo Shoots - As described by Cai Lun in 105 CE.jpg/Unknown author from the time of Ming dynasty / Public domain/wikimedia commons; 10b2/File:Five Steps of Papermaking - Step 2 - Pressing the Paper - As described by Cai Lun in 105 CE.jpg/Unknown author from the time of Ming dynasty / Public domain/wikimedia commons; 10b3/File:Five Steps of Papermaking - Step 3 - Pressing the Paper - As described by Cai Lun in 105 CE.jpg/Unknown author from the time of Ming dynasty / Public domain/wikimedia commons; 10b4/File:Five Steps of Papermaking - Step 4 - Pressing the Paper - As described by Cai Lun in 105 CE.jpg/Unknown author from the time of Ming dynasty / Public domain/wikimedia commons; 11tr/File:Hero of Alexandria Wellcome M0004255.jpg/See page for author / CC BY (https://creativecommons.org/licenses/by/4.0)/wikimedia commons; 11cl/File:Fotothek df tg 0000064 Architektur ^ Geometrie ^ Konstruktion ^ Gefäßkonstruktion ^ Dampfkugel ^ Windku.jpg/Deutsche Fotothek / Public domain/wikimedia commons; 12c/File:"The School of Athens" by Raffaello Sanzio da Urbino.jpg/Raphael / Public domain/wikimedia commons; 13tr/File:Mauryan coin with arched hill symbol on reverse.jpg/Classical Numismatic Group, Inc. http://www.cngcoins.com / CC BY-SA (http://creativecommons.org/licenses/by-sa/3.0/)/wikimedia commons; 13cr/File:Arthashastra.jpg/timsee / CC BY-SA (https://creativecommons.org/licenses/by-sa/4.0)/wikimedia commons; 13cl/File:Artgate Fondazione Cariplo - Cifrondi Antonio, Euclide.jpg/Fondazione Cariplo / CC BY-SA (https://creativecommons.org/licenses/by-sa/3.0)/wikimedia commons; 13bl/File:Caullery-Sémiramis.jpg/Attributed to Louis de Caullery / Public domain/wikimedia commons; 14cr/File:Jar with two handles, excavated in Cyprus, Iron Age, 8th-6th century BC, painted earthenware - Tokyo National Museum - Tokyo, Japan - DSC08534.jpg/Daderot / Public domain/wikimedia commons; 14bl/File:Exekias Dionysos Staatliche Antikensammlungen 2044.jpg/Exekias / CC BY-SA (http://creativecommons.org/licenses/by-sa/3.0/)/wikimedia commons; 17tr/File:Knochenleim Granulat.jpg/Simon Eugster – Simon / ?! 12:57, 8 May 2008 (UTC) / CC BY-SA (http://creativecommons.org/licenses/by-sa/3.0/)/wikimedia commons; 18tr/File:Clothes of Ötzi, Naturhistorisches Museum Wien.jpg/Sandstein / CC BY (https://creativecommons.org/licenses/by/3.0)/wikimedia commons; 18cl/File:Felt hat from Loulan. Early Han 202 BCE - 8 CE.jpg/John Hill / CC BY-SA (https://creativecommons.org/licenses/by-sa/3.0)/wikimedia commons; 18cr/File:Kirghiz shifting felt tent at Gumbaz-Ötek.png/Aurel Stein / Public domain/wikimedia commons; 19t/Meyers b10 s0120a.jpg/Bibliographisches Institut, Leipzig / Public domain/wikimedia commons; 19br/File:Drop spindle from Egypt.jpg/Peter van der Sluijs / CC BY-SA (https://creativecommons.org/licenses/by-sa/3.0)/wikimedia commons; 20cl/File:Makedonische phalanx.png/F. Mitchell, Department of History, United States Military Academy / Public domain/wikimedia commons; 20bl1/File:Alexander troops beg to return home from India.jpg/Antonio Tempesta / Public domain/wikimedia commons; 20bl2/File:Roman Army & Chariot Experience, Hippodrome, Jerash, Jordan (5072083097).jpg/yeowatzup / CC BY (https://creativecommons.org/licenses/by/2.0)/wikimedia commons; 20br/File:Side b of body of herakles neck amphora.jpg/Attributed to a painter of the Princeton Group / CC0/wikimedia commons; 21tl/File:Tapestry depicting the huntress Diana.jpg/Château de Villandry / Public domain/wikimedia commons; 21tr/File:Composite Bow with Forty Arrows MET DP165527.jpg/Metropolitan Museum of Art / CC0/wikimedia commons; 21cr/File:The Pharaoh Tutankhamun destroying his enemies.jpg/Unknown author / Public domain/wikimedia commons; 21bl/File:Ethunu kaduwa.jpg/Angampora / CC BY-SA (https://creativecommons.org/licenses/by-sa/3.0)/wikimedia commons; 21br/File:NarmerPalette ROM.jpg/Captmondo / Public domain/wikimedia commons; 21b/File:Kumsvärd. Early Scandinavian Bronze Age sword.jpg//wikimedia commons; 22tl/File:Warring states repeating crossbow.jpg/Yprpyqp / CC BY-SA (https://creativecommons.org/licenses/by-sa/4.0)/wikimedia commons; 22cr/File:Roman caltrop.jpg/Photographed by User:Bullenwächter / CC BY-SA (https://creativecommons.org/licenses/by-sa/3.0)/wikimedia commons; 22bl/File:Temporary exhibition about WWI, gare de Paris-Est, 2014 (caltrops).jpg/Tangopaso / Public domain/wikimedia commons; 23tr/File:Tut bumerangs.JPG/Dr. Günter Bechly / CC BY-SA (https://creativecommons.org/licenses/by-sa/3.0)/wikimedia commons; 23cr/File:Ballista (PSF).png/Pearson Scott Foresman / Public domain/wikimedia commons; 24tr/File:Sin-kashid cone (sikkatu), c. 1850 BC - Oriental Institute Museum, University of Chicago - DSC07176.JPG/Daderot / CC0/wikimedia commons; 24cl/File:Xerxes Cuneiform Van.JPG/Bjørn Christian Tørrissen / CC BY-SA (https://creativecommons.org/licenses/by-sa/3.0)/wikimedia commons; 24bl/File:Shang dynasty inscribed tortoise plastron.jpg/National Museum of China / CC BY-SA (https://creativecommons.org/licenses/by-sa/3.0)/wikimedia commons; 24br/File:Tablet V of the Epic of Gilgamesh.jpg/Osama Shukir Muhammed Amin FRCP(Glasg) / CC BY-SA (https://creativecommons.org/licenses/by-sa/4.0)/wikimedia commons; 24&25bg/Papyrus paper, abstract texture background. Papyrus was used in an ancient Egypt either painted the hieroglyphs or inscribed them with a reed pen on rolls of papyrus, the antecedent of our paper./William Potter/wikimedia commons; 25c/File:Odyssey manuscript.jpg/[1] (uploaded by Odysses) / Public domain/wikimedia commons; 25cr/File:Cheshm manuscript.jpg/wikimedia/wikimedia commons; 25bl/File:Code of Hammurabi 65.jpg/Rein Coppens / CC BY (https://creativecommons.org/licenses/by/2.0)/wikimedia commons; 26c/South-pointing_chariot_(Science_Museum_model)/Andy Dingley / CC BY (https://creativecommons.org/licenses/by/3.0)/wikimedia commons; 26bl/Model Si Nan of Han Dynasty.jpg//wikimedia commons; 27tl/File:Ancient obsidian arrowhead - Big Valley, California - 19 Oct. 2013.jpg/Darron Birgenheier from Reno, NV, USA / CC BY-SA (https://creativecommons.org/licenses/by-sa/2.0)/wikimedia commons; 27tr/Egyptian_Coffin_Mask/PericlesofAthens at English Wikipedia / CC BY-SA (http://creativecommons.org/licenses/by-sa/3.0/)/wikimedia commons; 27bl/File:Glass flask MET DP108415.jpg/Metropolitan Museum of Art / CC0/wikimedia commons; 27br/File:Egyptian Miniature Glasswares.jpg/PericlesofAthens at English Wikipedia / CC BY-SA (http://creativecommons.org/licenses/by-sa/3.0/)/wikimedia commons; 28tl/File:Fertile Crescent map.png/User:NormanEinstein / CC BY-SA (http://creativecommons.org/licenses/by-sa/3.0/)/wikimedia commons; 28c/File:Mahmoud Abbas Zieneldien.jpg/Mahmoud Abbas Zieneldien / CC BY-SA (https://creativecommons.org/licenses/by-sa/4.0)/wikimedia commons; 28 & 29 bottom background/File:The dawn of civilization- Egypt and Chaldaea (1897) (14577028168).jpg/Maspero, G. (Gaston), 1846-1916 / No restrictions/wikimedia commons; 29tl/File:Hama-3 norias.jpg/Heretiq / CC BY-SA (http://creativecommons.org/licenses/by-sa/3.0/)/wikimedia commons; 29cl/File:Chadouf égyptien, dessin de voyageur de 1890..jpg/G. Pearson / Public domain/wikimedia commons; 29bc/File:PSM V38 D177 A trip hammer.jpg/William F. Durfee / Public domain/wikimedia commons; 30bl/File:Baking mold Mari Louvre AO18902.jpg/Louvre Museum / Public domain/wikimedia commons; 30br/File:FuneraryModel-BakeryAndBrewery MetropolitanMuseum.png/Keith Schengili-Roberts / CC BY-SA (https://creativecommons.org/licenses/by-sa/2.5)/wikimedia commons; 31tr/File:Image-Zigong Salt.jpg/Phreakster 1998 at the English language Wikipedia / CC BY-SA (http://creativecommons.org/licenses/by-sa/3.0/)/wikimedia commons; 31b/File:Piles of Salt Salar de Uyuni Bolivia Luca Galuzzi 2006 a.jpg/Luca Galuzzi (Lucag), edit by Trialsanderrors / CC BY-SA (https://creativecommons.org/licenses/by-sa/2.5)/wikimedia commons;

Earth Discoveries

Shutterstock: 3b/Triff; 4&5bg/Magenta10; 5tr/Everett Collection; 5bl/Yevgenia Gorbulsky; 6tr/Takashi Images; 9bc/sisqopote; 11tl/Everett Historical; 12tr/TierneyMJ; 17bc/Zack Frank; 18tl/JuliusKielaitis; 18cl/buteo; 19tl/Tomas Kotouc; 19tr/FOTOGRIN; 20br/GUDKOV ANDREY; 21cr1/Bangweulu Lake - Image/SA-Pictures/; 21cr2/Alvaro Villanueva; 21bc/Stocksnapper; 22bl/REEDI; 25tr/Diego Grandi; 25bc/Don Mammoser; 25br/Bryan Busovicki; 30t/inigocia; 30cl/Vadim Petrakov; 30cr/Sunil Onamkulam; 30bl/my-summit; 30br/Alexey Kamenskiy; 31cr/Martin M303

Wikimedia Commons: 4b/# Route_of_Marco_Polo map/SY / CC BY-SA (https://creativecommons.org/licenses/by-sa/4.0)/wikimedia commons; 4tr/Marco_Polo_Mosaic_from_Palazzo_Tursi/Salviati / Public domain/wikimedia commons; 5cr/Kublai_Khan_square/Anige of Nepal - an astronomer, engineer, painter and confidant of Kublai Khan. / Public domain/wikimedia commons; 5br/FraMauroDetailedMapInverted//wikimedia commons; 6cr/ZhengHeShips/Not available; not given by uploader / Public domain/wikimedia commons; 6bl/File:Admiral Zhenghe.jpg/jonjanego / CC BY (https://creativecommons.org/licenses/by/2.0)/wikimedia commons; 6br/Kunyang_-_Zheng_He_Park_-_P1350545/User:Vmenkov / CC BY-SA (https://creativecommons.org/licenses/by-sa/3.0)/wikimedia commons; 7cr/Chen_Zhang's_painting_of_a_giraffe_and_its_attendant/Chen Zhang (陳璋) / Public domain/wikimedia commons; 7cl/Stamps_of_Indonesia,_026-05/Post of Indonesia / Public domain/wikimedia

Electronics & Communications

Inventions in Motion

Medical Inventions